GROUNDED IN LOVE

Advance Praise for
Grounded in Love

"Nancy Roth's ministry can be characterized by the word 'integrity;' integrity of body and spirit, and now integrity of humankind understood within rather than apart from the world God made and sustains. I thank her for this contribution to the most important work of our time."

—Marc Handley Andrus, Episcopal Bishop
of the Diocese of California

"Grounded in Love is a necessary antidote to our current fast-paced society, encouraging us to "listen with the ear of our heart" and take time to notice the natural world and celebrate our place in it. At the same time, this important book calls us to move from reflection to action—to live into our responsibility as people of faith to be good stewards of the environment."

—LeeAnne Beres, Executive Director,
Earth Ministry [Seattle, WA]

"This immensely alluring book is a spiritual invitation into a deeper experience of intentional life lived in awareness of the real world around us. It helps us to identify points of relationship and gives us time to pray and ponder what that has to teach us about who we are, why we are, and how creation is part of that answer."

—The Rt. Rev. Steven Charleston
President and Dean, Episcopal Divinity School

"The Rev. Nancy Roth gets at the big questions here—and it is just the right moment. Christians in our era will be judged by how they respond to the ecological crisis we now face, a crisis grounded in our consumerist materialism and taking its heaviest toll on the poorest and weakest on our planet. It's time to snap out of our trance and do something meaningful, and studying this book is a good place to start."

—Bill McKibben, author of The Comforting
Whirlwind: God, Job, and the Scale of Creation

"[*Grounded in Love*] summons us to a profound transformation, but one rooted in the ordinary which makes it both accessible and revolutionary....The Rev. Nancy Roth calls us to life and helps us know how to make that choice daily in ways simple, profound, and reverent."

—From the Foreword by David W. Orr, Paul Sears
Distinguished Professor of Environmental Studies, Oberlin College

"Nancy Roth invites us to recall and renew our love for all creation, because love, not guilt or obligation, is the motive that empowers action for the long run. Read, meditate, sing, dance, rejoice—and above all, love this world as together we work for the healing of our damaged creation."

—The Very Rev. Ward B. Ewing, D.D., Dean and President,
The General Theological Seminary of the Episcopal Church

"Roth, much-loved priest and trusted explicator of the way of prayer, is in every way the incarnation of the title she has chosen to use for her newest book, *Grounded in Love*, Roth's gentle commentary and her elegant passion entice us to a one-ness with creation and each other that is both active and rooted in faith."

—Phyllis Tickle, compiler, *The Divine Hours* and
The Words of Jesus—A Gospel of the Sayings of Our Lord

"Nancy Roth's new book breathes new hope into a renewal of reverence for all life on Earth. Her sacred scripture and art references enable the reader to see, hear, taste, and feel the beauty in the eco-systems that need dynamic care and better conservation."

—Joyce Wilding, ECUSA Province IV
Environmental Ministry Leader and Third Order Franciscan

"There is a language with which Earth's creatures address God. This language is nocturnal and diurnal. It is blithe, polyphonous, frightening, beautiful, comical. It is fraught with choices leading to spiritual life or death. Nancy Roth has been meditating on the wild language, and has heard in it a way to help entire churches out of darkness."

—David James Duncan, author of
The River Why and *God Laughs & Plays*

"We are vigilant and careful of that which we regard as valued and precious. Our most wonderful gift is the universe—earth, sky, and sea—which sustains our human life. Nancy Roth inspires the reader to share in the care and preservation of the magnificent gift and to participate in repairing the ecological damage done. The invitation is both hopeful and holy."

—(The Rev.) David Bryan Hoopes OHC,
Superior, Order of the Holy Cross

"Beyond the changing of our minds about what caring for the world will demand lies the greater challenge—the opening of our eyes and our hearts to be with God actively in love with the world. Nancy Roth's vivid reflections, suggestions for prayer, and proposals for action will be a Godsend to those who are ready to commit themselves to this spiritual adventure"

—The The Rev. Martin L. Smith, author of
A Season for the Spirit and *Compass and Stars*

""In Grounded in Love, Nancy Roth offers the reader her personal companionship in the spiritual disciplines of environmental fidelity to God. By story and direction she guides us into a deeper awareness of all with which God is blessing us in the natural world, and leads us to 'ponder and pray' our way into a relationship with the creation that leads to conversion."

—The Rt. Rev. Mark Hollingsworth, Jr., Bishop of Ohio

"Nancy Roth crosses easily between the worlds of faith and reason. She does so as a woman uncompromising in her preservation of intuition, the arts and beauty. But she is obviously bold enough to claim her place in a world of imploding religious patriarchy only catching up with the devastation brought on by the American Dream. Her commentaries on the Ten Commandments and the power of the Shaker dance could only be written by someone whose life is itself a bridge between worlds."

—Sr. Miriam Therese MacGillis, Genesis Farm

OTHER BOOKS BY NANCY ROTH

We Sing of God: A Hymnal for Children
(co-edited with Robert N. Roth)

Praying: A Book for Children

A Closer Walk: Meditating on Hymns for Year A

Awake My Soul: Meditating on Hymns for Year B

New Every Morning: Meditating on Hymns for Year C

Praise My Soul: Meditating on Hymns

The Breath of God: An Approach to Prayer

An Invitation to Christian Yoga (book and CD)

Organic Prayer: a Spiritual Gardening Companion

Meditations for Choir Members

Tween Prayer

Spiritual Exercises: Joining Body and Spirit in Prayer

GROUNDED IN LOVE

ECOLOGY, FAITH, AND ACTION

Nancy Roth

Foreword by David W. Orr

KenArnoldBooks LLC
Portland, Oregon

BT
695.5
.R678
2008

Copyright 2008 by Nancy Roth

All rights reserved. Printed in the United States of America. No part
of this book may be used or reproduced in any manner whatsoever
without written permission except in the case of brief quotations
embodied in critical articles and reviews.

Library of Congress Control Number: 2008927437

Unsuccessful efforts have been made to secure permission to quote
from some of the epigraphs in this book. If you are a copyright holder
of any of these materials, please contact the publisher.

Published by KenArnoldBooks, LLC,
1330 SW 3rd Avenue, 810, Portland, OR 97201

ISBN: 978-0-9799634-4-5

www.kenarnoldbooks.com

To Christopher

ACKNOWLEDGEMENTS

I am grateful to David Orr, whose Environmental Studies course at Oberlin College helped me organize my thoughts about this subject; he also read the manuscript and provided the Foreword in the midst of his very busy life.

I would like also to pay tribute to the late Norman Care, whose class on Environmental Ethics provided me with further insights.

I am indebted to my husband Bob, for his editing skills, his patience, and his loving support, as I brought this book to birth.

Last but far from least, my heartfelt thanks go to our son Christopher, to whom this book is dedicated. He very generously spent many hours reading, critiquing, and proof-reading the manuscript. Most of all, however, his deep awareness of environmental stewardship has long set an example of what it means to be "grounded in love."

Contents

Foreword

David W. Orr

The writer of Deuteronomy says: "I call heaven and earth to witness against you today that I have set before you life and death, blessings and curses. Choose life so that you and your descendants may live,..." (Deut. 30:19) No generation before our own could feel the full, global, and permanent weight of those words, but we can. The science could not be clearer. The members of the Intergovernmental Panel on Climate Change (2007) say that we have a very narrow window to stop and then reverse the accumulation of heat-trapping gases in the atmosphere before we risk the demise of civilization. Nicholas Stern, in the most authoritative report ever on the economics of climate change (2007), similarly warns of thresholds beyond which effective action becomes increasingly unlikely and finally impossible. The thousand scientists who wrote The *Millennium Ecosystem Assessment Report* (2005), also warn of surprises and points of no return dead ahead related to the breakdown of entire ecosystems and the loss of species. We are the generation that will chose between life and death, but now on a planetary scale and for all that will be born or could have been born.

All true spirituality beckons us to fullness of life and hope, but that is not the drift of the present conversation about sustainability. Mostly, it has been about how to devise a smarter economics and better technology. Certainly we need a smarter economics, which is to say one that includes all the costs of what we do. And certainly we need better technology to harvest current sunlight and eliminate pollution. These, however, are necessary, not sufficient changes, and they are grounded in the faith that we might become smart enough to make end-runs around natural constraints imposed by entropy and ecology, as well as the limits imposed by our own ignorance. In no important way does this discourse challenge the deeper sources of our plight which have to do with human desires and intentions now warped by a century of sybaritic commercialism and militarism. The point is that we will have to want to do better for deeper and more profound reasons than those of self-interest alone. Dietrich Bonhoeffer, who had good reason to know, once observed that there was no such thing as "cheap grace." The same applies, I believe, to the effort to make the human presence on Earth sustainable. In contrast to a great deal of the happy talk of our time, I think it wise to assume that the transition ahead will be a demanding and perilous journey that will ask a great deal of us and those who will follow. We face nothing less than a struggle for life over death now on the scale of the whole Earth, and we will have to reach deeper to go higher.

There can be no technical solution to what is at root a spiritual problem, but there is an interesting convergence between our self-interest in survival and ethics. The journey to sustainability requires us to do what the wisest have always said that we ought to do, but now the same argument holds for more mundane reasons of self-interest as well. We will have to thirst for righteousness and justice if we wish merely to live. America represents the future that much of the world still aspires to, but our manner of living cannot be sustained either physically or spiritually. So, there is serious and necessary talk of global bargains that would level our carbon emissions to perhaps two tons per person per year. By contrast the average in the United States is twenty tons of CO_2 per person each year. But by the remorseless working out of big numbers, that level cannot be sustained. Nor should we wish that it could, for that number conceals the cold reality of wars and injustices required by a culture of mass consumption powered by ancient sunlight. Are we up to the challenge? Will we choose life? That is THE question of our age and there is no other remotely as important.

For the past fifteen years, I've been privileged to know the Rev. Nancy Roth and her husband Robert as neighbors, friends, and colleagues. Nancy is a renaissance woman: a musician, writer, dancer, and a priest in the Episcopal Church. She has written powerfully and eloquently about the intersection of prayer and the world of gardening, music, and everyday living. In *Grounded in Love* she summons us to a profound transformation, but one rooted in the ordinary which makes it both accessible and revolutionary. Like the writer of Deuteronomy, Nancy Roth calls us to life and helps us know how to make that choice daily in ways simple, profound, and reverent.

DAVID W. ORR is the Paul Sears Distinguished Professor of Environmental Studies, Oberlin College.

INTRODUCTION

In 1977, President Jimmy Carter warned the American people that the nation's energy appetite could lead to a catastrophe: "We must not be selfish or timid if we hope to have a decent world for our children and grandchildren." He was widely ridiculed when he called the difficult effort ahead "the moral equivalent of war."[1] Only now, more than thirty years later, are we beginning to take the issues seriously about which Carter was so prescient. The reasons for this lag are found in the lack of our will to change, rather than in the lack of appropriate technologies.

That is why I called this book *Grounded in Love: Ecology, Faith, and Action,* for I believe that the future well-being of planet Earth is dependent on the human will. I also believe that becoming aligned with truth rather than falsehood, with altruism rather than selfishness, and with action rather than passivity, is good for the soul.

Grounded in Love has a dual purpose: to provide knowledge, and to inspire reflection. The book is intended to be read in the spirit of meditation and prayer. I begin each chapter with a quotation, usually from the spiritual tradition, and conclude with "Ponder and Pray": exercises intended to help integrate the content of the chapter with the reader's own life. I hope that my readers will include not only members of faith communities but also seekers who are not aligned with any specific religious institution. I hope that the book will reach environmentalists who seek a spirituality to undergird and energize their work, as well as people of faith who wish to move beyond the cultural disconnection with the natural world in order to find in the earth itself a rich source of meaning.

There has been a dearth of this kind of integration of the spiritual, the ethical, and the practical; I hope to fill the void, both for individuals and for spiritual leaders, for whom these pages contain concepts and language that will be of use in preaching, teaching, and worship, as well as for the decisions and activities of ordinary daily life.

Grounded in Love is also intended for use by study groups. Its five sections–"Love," Concern," "Ethics," "Action," and "Hope," each consisting of a number of short essays–make it usable for a five-week series. For clergy and lay leaders, I hope that the book will contribute to education about environmental issues. It can also be used as a structure for a retreat, workshop, or quiet day–in fact, much of this material grew out of my own experience of leading just such programs around the country.

This enterprise is grounded in, and thus begins with, *Love*–love for those who will follow us, as well as love for the natural world–which is why the first chapters in this book address the human heart.

Love makes us vulnerable to suffering, so readers are invited next to look clearly at their *Concern*. How do the "inconvenient truths" that are now being brought to our attention affect our spirits?

We are healthiest when our discomfort inspires us

to take action. We look next at our *Ethics:* what ecological principles help to guide our action? I explore how we can best interpret the great commandment to love God, neighbor, and self, in our present day. It has also been fascinating to look at these basic principles in tandem with the values embedded in the law given Moses on Sinai. In fact, I have organized the final ten chapters of this section as a kind of ecological *midrash*, or commentary, on the Ten Commandments.

The book moves on to the theme of *Action.* I provide a few examples of the way the principle of ecological design (which might well be considered the "great commandment" of environmental ethics) can be embodied in our buildings, our transportation, and our life-styles. There is no way that this section could be exhaustive in a book of this nature; the reader can seek such information elsewhere. I have contented myself with using a few lively and personal stories, intended to help you discover both the simple actions and sustainable technologies that can express your will to heal rather than harm God's creation.

It is not only because of my temperament, but because of my faith, that I conclude this book with *Hope.* For one thing, we are not alone: and, although we are working toward a "new world," our venture is nothing new. There is an ancient consciousness at work here: spiritual ancestors who can become our companions. There are also the children we raise and teach; they can, in turn, raise our consciousness and become themselves our best teachers. There are others who express, not through words, but through their arts, the life-giving sense of beauty that can be found through deep connection with the natural world. And there are all the ways we can seek inner transformation and consecrated action through our prayer, whether in words, reflection, deep silence, or action. For if we undertake this journey with God, we will walk in the close presence of the One whose love pervades the universe, and who, we trust, will bless each effort, large or small, to protect the divine creation.

LOVE

*I pray that...God may grant that you may be strengthened
in your inner being with power through the Spirit, and that
Christ may dwell in your hearts through faith, as you are being rooted and grounded in love.*

(Ephesians 3:16-17)

How do we "ground in love" our relationship to the
earth which is our home? It begins, I believe, with tending the "inner being" of which the writer of the Epistle to
the Ephesians speaks. This requires taking time to truly see,
whether we are looking at an infant cradled in our arms, the
starry night sky, a bright snowscape, or the iridescent body
of a beetle. As we lose ourselves in such contemplation, we
find ourselves as well, for we are coming home—both to our
childhood as creatures of earth, and to our Origin: the Creator of all that we gaze upon

1. KATRINA AND ANNA

Let me respectfully remind you:
Life and Death are of supreme importance.
Time swiftly passes by and opportunity is lost.
Each of us should strive to awaken,
Awaken,
Awaken.
Take heed.
Do not squander your life

—Evening Gatha (Buddhist)

Although the thoughts in this volume are the fruit of many years of experience, study, and reflection, my passion for gathering them into this book can be dated to a week toward the end of September, 2005. In my role as chaplain to the spouses of the bishops of the Episcopal Church, I had traveled to San Juan, Puerto Rico, to attend the bishops' autumn meeting. We all still were reeling from the images of the devastation and suffering in Louisiana and Mississippi due to Hurricane Katrina. First on the agenda were reports from the Gulf coast about the disaster and the subsequent relief efforts, bringing us face to face with images of death and loss. I had once learned that hurricanes serve the beneficial function of moving hot tropical air to the north and thus moderating the earth's climate. This provided little comfort, but Katrina *did* serve another ultimately very useful function. She forced the world to look at the reality of poverty and racism in the richest country in the world. Her fury brought to our consciousness fearful questions about the safety of human meddling with the ecosystem, a theme that was reiterated later in the day when the Bishop of Bangladesh came to the podium. Knowing that global warming contributed to rising sea levels as well as to Katrina's fury, he pleaded with the gathering, "Please use your power to convince those in high places to take action; otherwise my country could disappear in less than two decades."

I had decided to visit our son and his family in New Jersey on the way home to Ohio, because a second grandchild was expected at any moment–and, indeed, Anna entered the world just as I was landing at Newark Airport. I was not prepared for the emotional impact of a moment several days later. I was in grandparental bliss, rocking Anna, the first girl baby to arrive in our immediate family since my own birth. But in my head, instead of a lullaby, I heard the voice of the Bishop of Bangladesh.

And then I heard my own questions. What will the world be like when Anna and her big brother Gabriel grow up? Will they know the joy of swimming in clear water? Will they be able to hike in healthy forests, breathing fresh pine-scented air? Will the world be free from wars over the resources of oil and water? Will the world have moved closer to the ideal of justice and well-being for every member of the human race?

Or will the waters of the world be toxic, the forests depleted, the air unbreathable? Will our grandchildren's lives be made fearful by wars waged for the sake of diminishing supplies of oil or for the even more necessary resource of clean water? Will economic and social injustice cause ever more instability in the world? Will arrogance and fanaticism continue to breed terrorism? Will these grandchildren of ours be able to remain healthy, despite the toxins that they probably have already absorbed?

How best could I begin to contribute in at least a small way to a future world in which all human beings, from infants to the aged, might flourish? And where was God in this endeavor? I knew the answer, and have known it, in fact, for a long time, because I have been thinking about these issues for many years. I laid the groundwork in my volume *Organic Prayer* and in a few articles in religious journals. The gestation period for this book was long and full, and included sitting as an adult student in two environmental studies courses at Oberlin College. But it is the grandchildren who have provided me with the passion and the energy to fit the writing of *Grounded in Love* into my busy life.

As I held Anna or sat on the floor playing with Gabriel during the week after Anna's birth, I recognized that both my love for them and the foreboding I felt for their future were catalysts for action. That blend of love and concern contains the seeds of hope. They beckon us to choose between life and death–for ourselves, and for the children we love and their children and their children's children and all their descendants, as well.

In whatever way it happens to us, the journey towards hope begins with this strange mix of love and concern. We may take the very first step while holding a newborn soon after a devastating hurricane. We may take it when a friend is diagnosed with an environmentally-caused cancer. Or when a beloved landscape is forever changed because of melting glaciers or felled trees.

These experiences of love and concern remind us not to squander life—either our own or the lives of those who will come after us. God calls us to "Awaken, awaken, awaken!" acknowledging the truths that are so much a part of human existence at this time will be the catalyst for a journey of prayer and transformation, both for ourselves as individuals, and for our communities. This journey will take us into new territory, in which we learn to live more responsibly. In so doing, we will become more fully the images of God we were created to be, rejoicing in the abundance and beauty of creation, and devoting ourselves, with all our heart, our mind, and our strength to the vitality of life on earth.

Ponder and Pray

Take a few moments to relax and notice your breathing. Then visualize one or more of the young people you love. Picture them at the present time, full of life and promise. "Watch" them at play, and as they sleep.

Now see them in your mind's eye as they grow into adulthood. What kind of a world do you hope for them? Take some time to picture that world. "Choose life."

What kind of a world might they live in if the planet becomes less habitable? "Entertain the possibility of death." How does this possibility make you feel?

Now picture yourself converting the resulting discomfort into action, fueled by your desire to contribute to the future well-being of these children you love. Hold these children before God, as you inhale and exhale. As you inhale, welcome God's gift of life. As you exhale, picture yourself breathing forth God's healing upon the world these children will inherit from you.

2. Haunted Forever by the Eternal Mind

I am the one whose praise echoes on high.
I adorn all the earth.
I am the breeze that nurtures all things green.
I encourage blossoms to flourish with ripening fruits.
I am led by the spirit to feed the purest streams.
I am the rain coming from the dew
that causes the grasses to laugh with the joy of life.
I am the yearning for good.

—Hildegard of Bingen

When I was a senior at seminary, I decided to write a research paper on the subject of young children's earliest experiences of God. I began by interviewing some of my classmates. I asked them this question:

"What in your early childhood helped to shape your present sense of who God is, and how you relate to God? Your experiences might not have been identified at the time as 'religious'; however, they may have been early intimations of, for example, the 'otherness' of things, dependency, beauty, mystery, wholeness, etc."

It was extraordinary how many of my friends reported their first experiences of the "sacred" (for which, as young children, they as yet had no name) in the world of nature.

"I remember, when we lived in Alabama, coming home across the fields in the morning sunlight, and feeling an explosion of joy in the world's beauty; I would fling out my arms and sing, 'O, what a beautiful morning!'"

"What I remember so vividly is that nature was animate; it had a personality, and an immediacy. It had a distinctiveness as I was distinct. When I put my hands against a tree, the touch was a 'communication' with another entity. I could be quiet for hours on end in the woods, watching the water in the brook. There was a place where the water in the brook was clear. I had a sense of its aliveness as I was alive. I can still feel the sensation of sunlight on my head."

"I remember a house my grandmother had in Rhode Island. There was a split-rail fence outside my window, and in the evening hour a small bird would come and sit on that fence and sing his song. I remember a sense of wonder and mystery about there being a place belonging to us to which something else–this bird–came. Nobody could plan the bird, nor the green grass behind it. It just came; it was *there*."

"I remember going to the beach with my cousins. There, in the enormous space among the sand dunes, we looked at the small things: little animals with lives of their own were walking on the sand which we walked on as if it were nothing. They made holes after the waves had washed over the sand. I couldn't imagine living there. It used to puzzle me how vastly different they were. When the waves came up, I had a tactile sensation of communication with the shore. When I stood there, with my ankles sinking deeper and deeper into the sand, I was stepping into what was going on there all the time. I would feel this also when we would–half in fear, half in delight–lie down on the water's edge and let the waves break over us."

"In my early childhood world, plants, trees, and flowers were all alive. Everything was alive. Everything was an extension of my own awareness. Certain great trees had numinous qualities, to be approached with awe and discretion. I talked with violets and buttercups I picked, carefully explaining our 'need' of them at home. Cresting the top of one particular windswept, sagebrush hill inevitably produced a strong sense of the uncanny, a breathless expectancy that the next instant I would move into another realm."

The poet William Wordsworth would have told my fellow-students that, as children, they were in touch with a reality that we often ignore when we are adults:

> Thou best Philosopher, who yet dost keep
> Thy heritage, thou Eye among the blind,
> That, deaf and silent, read'st the eternal deep,
> Haunted for ever by the eternal mind.[2]

The child's initial steps in the life of faith are similar to the early steps of humanity's own journey. *Homo sapiens* first experienced the divine through the natural world and its mysteries. The rising and the setting of the sun; its progressive departure as the days grew shorter, and its miraculous turnabout as it came back to warm the earth once again; the bison, deer, boar, and bears painted on the walls of ancient caves; sacred stones and stately trees–all were objects of wonder.

Wordsworth longs for the "natural piety" of childhood:

> There was a time when meadow, grove, and stream,
> The earth, and every common sight,
> To me did seem
> Apparelled in celestial light,
> The glory and the freshness of a dream.
> It is not now as it hath been of yore;—
> Turn whereso'er I may,
> By night or day,
> The things which I have seen I now can see no more.[3]

Perhaps you also felt a twinge of nostalgia as you read the poet's words and those of my classmates. Perhaps that twinge is a hint that you are missing out on something that is integral to your well-being, one that you never needed to leave behind in the first place. We do not outgrow our innate connection with the natural world, although we may have learned to ignore it. As we mature, the stages of our lives remain embedded within us, like the inmost pieces of twine on a ball of string. Our childhood is still there: not just a part of the whole that is oneself, but the very center.

The journey of the human race, as well as of individuals, begins with our earliest years, when we were "best philosophers." Our relationship with nature is a treasure buried deep within us. It can develop beyond the naiveté of childhood into a mature appreciation of the sacredness of God's creation. When we begin to unearth it, we discover new meaning, new delights, and new duties. When it comes to "choosing life," it is the first step–for ourselves and for our planet.

Ponder and Pray

Take some time to remember early memories of exploring nature, whether it was in a city park, at a beach, in your back yard, or in a woods or a meadow. What did you see? What did you hear? Were there interesting smells, like wild honeysuckle or the fishiness of a bay at low tide? Did you enjoy touching things like moss, or mud, or the cold water in a puddle?

How did you feel when there was thunder and lightening outside your bedroom window? When there was deep snow, or a day so hot that, if you went barefoot, the pavement hurt your feet? When it was autumn, and you jumped in piles of leaves? When the sky turned red and orange at sunset?

Did you feel pleasure, fear, excitement, a sense of belonging, a sense of wonder? Did these experiences make you feel very small? Did they make you feel connected to something bigger than you? What would you have responded if I had asked you the question I asked my seminary classmates: "What in your early childhood helped to shape your present sense of who God is, and how you relate to God?"

3. ECSTASY

The trees of the Holy One are full of sap,
The cedars of Lebanon which God planted,
In which the birds build their nests,
And in whose tops the storks make their dwellings....
O Holy One, how manifold are your works!
in wisdom you have made them all;
The earth is full of your creatures.

—*Psalm 104: 17-18, 25*[4]

I suppose that my love for birds was inspired by both my mother and my third-grade teacher, Miss Robinson. Even during World War II, when many foodstuffs were rationed, the cardinals, nuthatches, and chickadees could count on a daily banquet in our back yard, due to the stash of birdseed my mother kept in the garage. The feeder was placed outside the dining room window, in a direct line of vision from my assigned place at the dinner table. When I was six, Mother bought me a bright yellow canary, who used to sing whenever I practiced the piano. I named him Bing Crosby. We would release him every so often, giving him the freedom of the kitchen, but only much later would I begin to feel a twinge of sadness that he never knew life in the wild.

Miss Robinson made sure that all of the students in her classroom enrolled in the Junior Audubon Society. From then on, in addition to daily sessions dedicated to such academic pursuits as spelling, arithmetic, and geography, we spent part of each day studying two very large Audubon Society charts that hung on the classroom wall. We looked forward to the game of trying to identify each species. Robins we knew already, and cardinals. But we also learned to discover–nestled among the trees and undergrowth painted on the charts–nuthatches, chickadees, goldfinches, wrens, and other species we didn't even have in our yards. One of the easiest to find was the bright orange male oriole, which I had never seen "in person," although once my mother had pointed out its distinctive nest hanging from the limb of a tall tree.

Years later, when my husband and I moved into a house of our own, we followed the family tradition by purchasing a bird feeder. Many of the birds whose names I learned from the third-grade bird charts have flown into our back yard, the way they did in my childhood. We try to satisfy each avian taste by providing sunflower, safflower, thistle seeds, and suet cakes.

From time to time, I have also attached a wedge of orange to the feeder, hoping to attract a Baltimore oriole. The only result of my efforts was a series of dehydrated oranges, taken down with regret when, uneaten by any oriole, they became covered with ants.

But then, one day, he appeared, like a vision. The exquisite orange and black bird from Miss Robinson's bird chart was perched on the orange. I could hardly get out the words to my husband: "Bob...look!" The effect of that beauty on me was like an electrical charge, as if I had inadvertently come into contact with the household current or been struck by a bolt of lightning. But it was not only my body that was affected. The oriole, one of the loveliest of God's creatures, "charged" my psyche as well, like a visitation of the Spirit. The word that came to my mind was "ecstasy."

Ecstasy was the title that Bruce Wilshire, a professor of philosophy at Rutgers University, was considering for his book about the innate human need for contact with the natural world. He finally called it *Wild Hunger: The Primal Roots of Modern Addiction.*[5] "Human life," he says, "was formed through millions of years in which our human and prehuman ancestors survived only by coping with wild Nature....Even when terrified at times, they probably did not feel emotionally empty. I strongly suspect that on one level we still hunger for primal excitement, but the hunger is partially suppressed and confused by overlayings of later agricultural, industrial, and now electronic life."

The gratifications we try to substitute for this experience of nature can never be sufficient. These substitutes, repeated slavishly, become addictions. What is the solution? Wilshire sums it up: "Awe undermines addictions." *Awe undermines addictions!*

The Greek roots of the word "ecstasy" mean "a standing out" from the space that one's body occupies, as if our very being were caught up in the surrounding world. For Wilshire, experiences of ecstasy serve a primal need: "to *be* fully through time...to progressively discover our being in the wide world, not just to have it, as if it were a possession."

Discovering our being in the wild world brings us the pleasure of moving outside of ourselves, through awe or through–even more potent–ecstasy. For Wilshire, this experience is found through our connection with nature. Theologians would say it is found through our connection with God, which is why the best-known artistic depiction of ekstasis is Bernini's statue of St. Teresa of Avila, dissolving in joy.

I would say it is not a question of "either/or," but of "both/and," for the natural world is an expression of God. "O Holy One, how manifold are your works! In wisdom you have made them all; the earth is full of your creatures."

How do we discover our right relation with the works of God in nature? My fellow seminary students remembered that in childhood they experienced the numinous in nature and only later identified that experience with God. In adulthood we may need to go through the process the other way around, understanding once again the connection of the Creator with the creation.

This is different from "pantheism," the belief that God is contained *only* in nature. (An example is the nature-worship of our earliest ancestors.) Instead, this is "pan*en*theism," the term the theologian Jürgen Moltman used to describe the transcendent God's immanence in the world. The Christian sees God in nature, but not only in nature.

When we can sing with all our hearts, "O Holy One,

how manifold are your works!" it will be the beginning of healing not only for our world, but for ourselves.

Ponder and Pray

Find a quiet, comfortable place in which to spend some time praying Psalm 104, which is printed in its entirety in this book's Appendix (p.245). Read each verse of the psalm slowly. Pause and close your eyes after each verse. Try to picture the image that you have just read, as if you were actually seeing it. "See" God wrapped with light as with a cloak, the mountain goats on the high hills, the lions roaring after their prey, the Leviathan "made for the sport of it."

Now go outdoors–or, if the weather does not cooperate, look out your window to the world outside. (Even in a city, there is the sky. And you can include the people you see, for we are also a part of the natural world : "We go forth to our work and to our labor until the evening"!) Either silently or aloud, say the psalm in your own way, naming what you see. For example, "O Holy One, how manifold are your works! In wisdom you have made them all; the earth is full of your creatures. There is the soft-falling snow, creating a blanket for the garden. Yonder is the small grey squirrel, leaping from branch to branch of the oak. There is the faithful mail deliverer, making his daily visit to our house in every kind of weather...."

4. Stars

*We had the sky, up there, all speckled with stars, and we used
to lay on our backs and look up at them, and discuss about
whether they was made, or only just happened.*

—*Mark Twain, Huckleberry Finn*

Stars, when we take time to look at them, put us in our
place. I discovered this phenomenon in childhood, when my
parents regularly took my brothers and me to the Hayden
Planetarium in New York City. I always looked forward
to tipping back my upholstered seat as the lights dimmed
and "stars" began to prick through the midnight blue ceiling high above me. I remember the extraordinary calm and
happiness that settled over me as the constellations moved
across the domed ceiling.

No longer was my attention focused upon my self or my
childhood worries. Instead, I found myself absorbed in a
mystery so much vaster than the small universe of my own
life that it felt as if my brain itself had been altered. For
once, I knew self-forgetfulness. Strangely, I also discovered
a sense of belonging. I felt both very small and very large,
part of the vastness of the pattern above me.

Since Thomas Edison, there are not many places one
can see such a sky, although I once stayed in a hermitage
perched above St. Benedict's Abbey in Snowmass, Colorado,
where the blaze of the night sky made me reluctant to close

my eyes in sleep. Van Gogh has captured such a sky in one of my favorite paintings, *The Starry Night,* where the stars swirl with energy above the dark cypresses and shadowy roofs of a village. Standing in front of that painting recently in New York's Museum of Modern Art, I felt myself almost swept physically into the painting. No wonder that the artist wrote: "I have...a terrible need...shall I say the word?...of religion. Then I go out at night and paint the stars."[6] I *hear* similar stars in Haydn's oratorio *The Creation,* when, after a tenor solo ending with, "He made the stars also," a single violin spins out a note, *pianissimo,* and one by one other instruments join it, until there is a blaze of sound.

The stars help me to understand time differently. What I am seeing–because their light takes so long to reach the earth–is actually time past: stars as they existed many years ago. The closest star beyond our Sun is 4.2 light-years away (about twenty-four trillion miles), but most are much further; light from the farthest object we can see with the naked eye, the Andromeda Galaxy, has taken three million years to reach us. The night sky helps me to relax about my own place in time, as I grasp, ever so tentatively, what eternity might mean.

I like to think that the stars hovering over Nazareth and Bethlehem long ago, or over our own homes today, are the same stars flung across the sky from God's hand at the beginning of time, according to the Hebrew creation story. Should I return to the planetarium, however, I would learn that it only looks that way to us. The stars have not always been there, but were formed well after the Big Bang–a term I understand as science's way of describing the action of the hand of God. Although the stars look constant, they are born and they die, sometimes giving birth to offspring in their death, like the Sun on which we so much depend. Their life cycles are so much longer than our own that we never notice the change. It takes a phenomenon like a comet, a supernova, or the Star of Bethlehem to draw our attention to the fact that even the stars in the present night sky are in flux. For the most part, we are content to gaze at them in wonder; it is their beauty itself that is unchanging.

That is, when we can see them! One of the unfortunate legacies of the discovery of electricity is light pollution. When I was young, my parents explained to me that the reddish glow in the night sky came from New York City, twenty miles away. The glow obscured many of the stars I would otherwise have seen–which is probably why the planetarium's sky made such an impression. Not too long ago, our small Ohio town estimated the potential effects of a Wal-Mart Superstore to be built a couple of miles to the south of us. A professor in Oberlin College's astronomy department campaigned to reduce the height and the wattage of the lights in its giant parking lot, and succeeded: a small victory for the stars.

I like to think that the Trappist monk and author Thomas Merton had been pondering the brilliant night sky above his hermitage in the Kentucky countryside when he wrote:

For the world and time are the dance of the Lord in emptiness. The silence of the spheres is the music of a wedding feast. The more we persist in misunderstanding the phenomena of life, the more we analyze them out into strange finalities and complex purposes of our own, the more we involve ourselves in sadness, absurdity and despair. But it does not matter much, because no despair of ours can alter the reality of things or stain the joy of the cosmic dance that is always there. Indeed, we are in the midst of it, and it is in the midst of us, for it beats in our very blood, whether we want it to or not.[7]

Whether Merton knew it or not, science would have supported that claim. The energy of the Big Bang produced hydrogen, helium, and trace amounts of lithium; from that gas and dust came the stars, from which came the heavier elements, and then the earth, and, finally, ourselves. In a sense, through us creation looks back upon itself. The stars beat in our very blood, as we earthlings step outside at night for a breath of fresh air. It is no wonder they calm us, for we are looking at our origins; from stardust, everything on our planet was created. I still love the theological truth of the Hebrew creation story in which God, the sculptor, picks up dust "from the ground" and breathes life into it. But our real origin is both more complicated and more wondrous than that. We are not merely part of the earth; we are part of the cosmic beauty we see above us.

Despite everything–our anxieties, preoccupations, illnesses, losses–this beauty remains, constant as God's presence. Perhaps our best acknowledgment of that fact would be to step outdoors each evening when the sky is clear, and simply look up.

Ponder and Pray

All world religions have creation stories that communicate truths about ourselves and our relationships with the natural world and other human beings. In our day, we are privileged to have also a "common creation story," thanks to the scientific community. Here is a summary of that story, taken from the book *The Universe is a Green Dragon*, written by the physicist Brian Swimme. The story is told in the context of an imaginary conversation between a youth and Thomas Berry, a Roman Catholic theologian, ecologist, and cultural historian.

As with the two biblical creation stories in the beginning chapters of Genesis, this one provides much food for reflection and meditation. Take some time to read this story, and to reflect upon it.

Youth: Where should we start?

Thomas: We need to start with the story of the universe as a whole. Our emergent cosmos is the fundamental context for all discussions of value, meaning, purpose, or ultimacy of any sort. To speak of the universe's origin is to bring to mind the great silent fire at the beginning of time.

Imagine that furnace out of which everything came forth.

21

This was a fire that filled the universe–that was the universe. Every point of the cosmos was a point of this explosion of light. And all the particles of the universe churned in extremes of heat and pressure, all that we see about us, all that now exists was there at the beginning, in that great burning explosion of light.

Youth: How do we know about it?

Thomas: We can see it! We can see the light from the primeval fireball. Or at least the light from its edge, for it burned for nearly a million years. We can see the dawn of the universe because the light from its edge reaches us only now, after traveling twenty billion years to get here....

Most amazing is this realization that every thing that ex-ists in the universe came from a common origin. All the material of your body and the material of my body are intrinsically related because they emerged from and are caught up in a single energetic event. Our ancestry stretches back through the life forms and into the stars, back to the beginnings of the primeval fireball. This universe is a single multiform energetic unfolding of matter, mind, intelligence, and life. And all of this is new. None of the great figures of human history were aware of this. Not Plato, or Aristotle, or the Hebrew Prophets, or Confucius, or Thomas Aquinas, or Leibniz, or Newton, or any other world-maker. We are the first generation to live with an empirical view of the origin of the universe. We are the first humans to look into the night sky and see the birth of stars, the birth of galaxies, the birth of the cosmos as a whole. Our future as a species will be forged within this new story of the world.[8]

What feelings does this story evoke in you? If you have a journal, write down some of the thoughts it has inspired.

5. MOUNTAINS AND CANYONS

You ask
why I perch
on a jade green mountain?
I laugh
but say nothing
my heart
free
like a peach blossom
in the flowing stream
going by
in the depths
in another world
not among men.

—Li Po[9]

Many years ago, using as our bible a book entitled *Europe on Five Dollars a Day*, we took our two young sons to Europe. Friends had recommended Wengen, a village nestled in the shadow of the Jungfrau, so we decided to spend a week there. We hiked the mountain trails and, on Sunday, rode the ski-lift up to a café where the villagers danced to the music of a Swiss band punctuated by the bells of dairy cows grazing in an adjacent meadow. One memorable day, we made an excursion to the Jungfrau. It involved a ride on a steep cog railway, the last part of which took us through a very dark tunnel. When we finally emerged at the observation center near the summit, we were practically blinded by the sun's brilliance. As our eyes began to adjust we could see that we were standing face to face–in German-speaking Switzerland–with a bronze plaque in *English*: "O Lord, how manifold are your works! In wisdom you have made them all." Someone, long ago, had responded to the incredible beauty of this place by deciding to remind future visitors of its source.

We spent a few hours in the rarified air, exploring the ice caves carved into the glacier and watching distant hikers climbing towards the peak. I more than once cautioned the children when they got too close to the edge of the abyss which lay below them. (Before the trip was over, they were to tell me, "Mother, we are never going to go to Switzerland with you again.")

When the sun dropped close to the horizon, we knew it was time to go, so we returned to the cog railway. The train platform was packed with very large and very aggressive tourists with enormous backpacks. They were all determined to board–and all at the same time. Our family was no match for them, and several trains came and left without us. Finally, I had reached the breaking point. When the next train arrived, I jumped on quickly and shouted, at the top of my voice, gesturing towards my family on the platform, "Mon mari et mes enfants!" with as much authority as I could muster. (I suppose I thought that, since I did not speak German, using any language other than English would draw attention.) Frightened by what they thought was a case of hysteria, a few people made way for us, and we were on our way down the mountain.

The juxtaposition of such beauty and such behavior haunted me. "O Lord, how manifold are your works!" Did this not include those two creatures in our care, who were only twelve and fifteen at the time, neither of them very hefty? I would like to think that the Jungfrau would have humbled others, as it had humbled us. But something stronger had taken over once those tourists had reentered the dim light of the cog railway station: an egocentricity that is, unfortunately, as much part of the human condition as is the capacity for humility and joy in God's works.

As I myself demonstrated, when I reached that breaking point, we all have the capacity to behave in either way. We can view the world through the very small lens of survival, or we can let a snow-clad mountain expand our view. Discovering–or rather rediscovering–"our being in the wide world" (in the words of Bruce Wilshire), can help us move from one towards the other, if we permit it to do so.

The experience of nature in its vastness can even transform our worry into wonder. The October after 9/11, we visited the Grand Canyon, at the invitation of some friends who were vacationing nearby. Our hearts were all beating a little faster during the anxious autumn months of 2001: the taste of fear was part of our daily experience. One day during our visit, I remember glancing at a newspaper at the lodge, where we were having breakfast, and seeing a headline with the word "nuclear" in it, which was more than enough to put me into survival mode.

After we had finished our coffee, we went outdoors into a landscape that is one of the wonders of the world. We watched colors change as the sun rose higher in the sky. As we walked along the rim, we came to a small stone visitor center perched on the edge, and there it was again: "O Lord, how manifold are your works! In wisdom you have made them all." As the sun rose higher, the heaviness in my heart was lifted. It wasn't because I had reasoned myself out of my fear. It was because the Grand Canyon had taken me out of myself, and also helped me find myself.

Thomas Berry is hopeful that humanity is moving in the right direction:

> We are returning to our native place after a long absence, meeting once again with our kin in the earth community. For too long we have been away somewhere, entranced with our industrial world of wire and wheels, concrete and steel, and our unending highways, where we race back and forth in continual frenzy.[10]

He compares this return to the poet Dante's meeting with Beatrice at the end of the *Purgatorio*. When he glimpses her approaching in a chariot filled with blossoms, the "ancient flame" of his youthful love for her comes to life again. Dante's epic, *The Divine Comedy (Commedia)*, is the story, not merely of the afterlife, but of his personal journey towards holiness, with all of his very human struggles. Berry believes that if Dante were writing in our day, he would include the need for the human community to reconcile with the divine presence in nature, after our long period of alienation. He suggests some avenues we could use:

> The world of life, of spontaneity, the world of dawn and
> sunset and glittering stars in the dark night heavens, the
> world of wind and rain, of meadow flowers and flow-
> ing streams, of hickory and oak and maple and spruce
> and pineland forests, the world of desert sand and prairie
> grasses, and within all this the eagle and the hawk, the
> mockingbird and the chickadee, the deer and the world and
> the bear, the coyote, the raccoon, the whale and the seal,
> and the salmon returning upstream to spawn–all this....[11]

As well as the Jungfrau and the Grand Canyon, of course!

Ponder and Pray

Find a position in which you can relax. Relax your body, thinking of releasing tension from each part of the body in turn. Notice that, although your body is at rest, it is likely that your head is full of irritating thoughts, what some call "monkey mind" or "mosquito mind."

Now think of the most dramatically beautiful place you have ever visited. It may be as well-known as the Jungfrau or the Grand Canyon. It may be a lake you have visited, or a view of the vast sky over the Great Plains. It may be an English garden, a forest near your home, or even a favorite tree, exquisitely shaped by wind and weather.

Picture this place as completely as you can. What colors are in the landscape, what objects? What does the sky look like? How does it feel to breathe the air? Are there any fragrances? Are there other people present? Take some time to dwell there in your imagination. If thoughts of other things come into your mind, just let those thoughts drift past like clouds and disappear. How do you feel? Are you letting go of some of your usual preoccupations? Are you feeling more peaceful? Does picturing this natural scene help you to leave behind the "continual frenzy" of life and "return to your native place after a long absence"?

6. Microcosmos

Apprehend God in all things,
for God is in all things.
Every single creature is full of God
and is a book about God.
Every creature is a word of God.
If I spent enough time with the tiniest creature,
even a caterpillar–
I would never have to prepare a sermon.
So full of God is every creature.

—Meister Eckhart (c.1260-1327)

When it came to butterflies, my classroom was the dentist's office. While I was having my teeth cleaned one day, Linda, the hygienist, mentioned casually, "My daughter raises monarchs." In a nation whose history began with a rebellion against a king, "monarchs" can mean only one thing. "How," I asked, "does she do it?" Linda answered, "First, she plants milkweed."

So the secret was a humble roadside plant. I had, on occasion, paid close attention to milkweed, not as a source of food for monarch butterflies, but as a visual prop for children's sermons. The most memorable example was in a suburban church. I had tucked a milkweed pod in a gift-wrapped box which, of course, they could hardly wait to unwrap. Inside, I told them, was a message about God. Before I knew it, tiny silken parachutes were sailing out over the congregation, a sign of the abundant divine love that pervades the world. Later, when I climbed up into the pulpit to preach a sermon for the adults, I saw the winged seeds still floating above the pews and the dark red carpet. I found myself grateful that I was leaving town before the sexton arrived to clean the church the following week–although, in retrospect, I realize that a better expression of spreading God's love would have been to offer to vacuum the carpet myself!

But I digress. Milkweed is much more than a useful symbol for a children's sermon; it is, in fact, an expression of God's love for the monarch. The caterpillar finds its leaves delicious, feasting on them in order to gather the energy to form the chrysalis chosen by the Greeks as an example of metamorphosis and by Christians as a sign of death and resurrection. Upon emerging, the butterfly's bright wings take it, along with thousands of other monarchs, south to Mexico's Sierra Madre or to the central and southern coast of California, where it spends the winter. In the spring, it heads north again, breeding along the way; and its offspring, by means of innate butterfly radar, return to the starting point.

"Would you like a milkweed plant?" Linda asked. Indeed, I would. I tucked it in among the wild flowers I had planted at the back of our property. Would just one plant suffice, if I also wanted to contribute to the monarch population? My answer came one day in the form of a caterpillar about two inches long, boldly striped in black, yellow, and white. Bending close, I found another. And another. I was "raising monarchs"! One day they were gone. I called Linda. Where might the chrysalises be? Hidden, she said, probably attached to a twig, or under a leaf. I never knew when the butterflies emerged, but in my imagination I saw them gathering with their counterparts from the fields and farms that surround this town and heading south.

It is quite easy to like butterflies, but often it is more difficult to feel affection for others of earth's smaller creatures. For consciousness-raising purposes, I can think of no better resource than a movie. *Microcosmos,* filmed by French cinematographers, welcomes us into the life of the "small cosmos" of a meadow in rural France. Its citizens include those I either overlook or brush away when I am outdoors. This film makes it impossible to ignore them, because skill, patience, and a very fine lens bring them into scale with our own larger world, as if we were Alice in Wonderland after we'd imbibed the shrinking potion. Small dramas unfold: a rainstorm, with drops of water the size of basketballs; two snails in a graceful mating dance set to music that bears a striking resemblance to Wagner's "Tristan and Isolde"; a dung beetle laboring to push what looks like a boulder impaled on a twig, eliciting applause from the movie audience when he finally figures out that he can succeed by pushing from another angle. The final image is of a beautiful creature emerging from a pond, unfolding its translucent wings, and taking flight. Afterwards, the cast of characters scrolls down the screen in the order of appearance. The final image, which had made us catch our breath, is...a mosquito!

It is no wonder that, when our son Christopher, who is attuned to this world, recommended this movie, he said, "It will change your attitude."

Christopher, a gardener, knows that we need these creatures. Many of them are pollinators, without whom we would not have apples, peaches, watermelons squash, cucumbers, or cherries. Many insects serve as food for other creatures, a function I am glad the mosquito serves, when I see bats sweeping low over a pond in the twilight. Some of them, especially the ants, aerate the soil, who, along with the earthworms, accomplish this much more efficiently than a mechanical rototiller.

These creatures can also serve the same function as stars, mountains, and canyons: they fill us with wonder, and thus help to teach us about our place on earth. The biologist E. O. Wilson writes: "The question I'm asked most often about ants is 'What do I do about the ones in my kitchen?' And my answer is always the same: 'Watch where you step.....Get a magnifying glass. Watch them closely.'[12]

Wilson tells us that ants "seized control" of a large part of earth long before the first primates walked the earth. Their success and longevity–around 100 million years–can teach us a great deal about working together as a species and celebrating our own humble yet significant place in the web of life. Ants are a part of the diversity of life on earth–a diversity crucial to the health of our planet, as well as to our own well-being.

Even Wilson's gentle bearing communicates this respect

for his favorite small creatures. He communicates it not only through the books he has written, but also in the signing of them. One day, after standing in line for his autograph, I handed him the book I had just purchased, and soon understood why the line had moved slowly: after he signed his name with a flourish, he took time to draw in my copy–meticulously, and with obvious affection—the image of an ant.

Ponder and Pray

Take some time to explore the "microcosmos."

In cold or inclement weather

Browse through a guide to insects or butterflies. I have a particular favorite, called *The Songs of the Insects,* which includes not only fine photographs but a CD of insect songs.[13]   When I play the CD in the middle of winter, I am transported to a summer meadow, despite the snow outside my window. The sounds are a rich source for meditation: sit quietly and just listen, letting your mind rest in the Creator's presence. The Hebrew word *anawim* describes those people who are the "overlooked" of society, but who teach important truths to the powerful. Thank God for these *anawim* of the microcosmos, upon whom so much of life depends.

In warm weather

Spend at least fifteen minutes outdoors in *one spot,* close to the ground, observing closely the life of the "microcosmos." If you have a magnifying glass, so much the better. Especially in the evening, *listen!* Read and meditate upon Emily Dickinson's poem about the diminutive songsters. (She uses the word "pathetic" to indicate that the insects aroused her feelings of sympathy and compassion):

> Farther in summer
> Than the birds
> Pathetic from the grass
> A minor nation celebrates
> Its unobtrusive mass.[14]

7. THE EARTH BALL

With my sight I returned through every one of the seven spheres, and I saw this globe such that I smiled at its paltry semblance....The little threshing-floor that makes us all so fierce all appeared to me from hills to river-mouths....

—Dante's view of Earth from: Commedia, Paradiso, Canto XXII

I was perusing a gift catalog in preparation for Christmas, when I spotted it: "The Earth Ball–The Astronaut's View from Space, Created with NASA Satellite Photos– $14.95 plus shipping." It is not often one can obtain such a perfect symbol for $14.95.[15]

I never tire of looking at it. It is fifty-two inches in circumference, just the right size to cradle in my arms. The accompanying pamphlet suggests that our world view inevitably changes when we actually view our planet in this way. Some of the quotations are from the past: "Humans must rise above the Earth...to the top of the atmosphere and beyond. For only thus will we understand the world in which we live." (Socrates, 400 B.C.); "Once a photograph of the Earth, taken from the outside, is available–a new idea as powerful as any in history will be let loose." (Fred Hoyle, British Astrophysicist, 1948)

There are also reflections from those in our own day who have been privileged to look back at our planet from outer space, a view that Dante was able only to imagine:

"The Earth was small, light blue, and so touchingly alone, our home that must be defended like a holy relic. The Earth was absolutely round. I believe that I never knew what the word Round meant until I saw the earth from space." (Aleksei A. Leonov, Voskhod 2, Soyuz 19-Epas).

"The first day or so we all pointed to our countries. The third or fourth day we were pointing to our continents. By the fifth day we were aware of only one earth." (Sultan Bin Salmon al-Saudi, Saudi Arabia, SS 5-G).

"Before I flew I was already aware of how small and vulnerable our planet is; but only when I saw it from space, in all its ineffable beauty and fragility, did I realize that humankind's most urgent task is to cherish and preserve it for future generations." (Sigmund Jahn, Germany, Soyuz 31)

And, finally: "Below was a welcoming planet. There, contained in the thin, moving, incredibly fragile shell of the biosphere is everything that is dear to you, all the human drama and comedy. That's where life is, that's where the good stuff is." (Loren Acton, USA, Challenger).

Compare these quotations with just one of the shocking yet hopeful facts inside the pamphlet—"The projected cost for global restoration of the environment has been estimated by the Worldwatch Institute to be only 15% of current world military spending." Our planet is indeed a "little threshing floor that makes us all so fierce."

No amount of preaching, especially that intended to induce guilt, will move us to action to change such priorities. Instead, our hearts need to be "strangely warmed" (in the celebrated words of John Wesley) by our personal relationship with nature and with God. It may happen through the ecstasy of spotting an oriole, the calm induced by gazing at the night sky, our awe in the presence of the immensity of a snow-covered glacier or deep red canyon, through the wonder of a close encounter with an ant—or, failing an opportunity to soar into space ourselves, simply holding an Earthball and pondering it.

Our relationship with nature and with God will shape our understanding of the world, inform our prayer, vitalize our action, and also help us discern our values. For Christians, our values are shaped by the teachings, life, and ministry of Jesus. But these values are not imposed upon us by God: we must freely choose them before we can willingly act upon them. The desire to be shaped by God is the beginning of our transformation, as we learn to respond to the "Love that moves the sun and the other stars," in the words of the poet Dante. In our time, it is imperative that we allow that Love to move *us* as well—the earthlings who live on this planet.

That Love will move us beyond our narrow definition of sin, for example—which traditionally has dealt only with the way we treat one another—to an increased understanding of our sin towards the planet itself. The two, of course, cannot be separated. Like the astronauts who first pointed to their own countries, then to their continents, and finally became aware of only one Earth, we will begin to understand that we are truly one human family. When we allow human activity to damage the Earth, we are placing humanity in jeopardy, not just the forests, oceans, and plains and their non-human denizens. Moreover, it is our poorest brothers and sisters–those people described by Jesus as the most beloved of God–who suffer more than anyone else when environmental disasters occur, whether they be drought, fire, hurricanes, or the poisoning of water and air.

We are not only being moved towards a broader understanding of what it means to live together on one planet, but towards a different understanding of time, as we consider our human brothers and sisters who will live in future centuries. Our actions will flow from these new understandings. As such, they will become "sacraments"–"outward and visible signs of inward and spiritual grace"–rather than mere duties. To my amusement, I glimpsed what that meant one day long ago, when I was tying up newspapers for recycling and discovered that the opening words of the ancient hymn called "St. Patrick's Breastplate" were ringing in my ears: "I bind unto myself today the strong name of the Trinity...." Recycling newspapers, of course, is a mere gesture towards planetary health, but, as my response to the Creator, it could even be considered an act of worship. And gestures add up. Gesture by gesture, sacramental act by sacramental act, we can become ever more the people who bind up the wounds of our planet in the strong name of the Trinity: the Creator who gave us this sweet earth; Jesus, who came to show us the way to love; and the Spirit who gives us strength and hope.

The pamphlet enclosed with the Earth Ball suggests some games children can play with it: Earth Volleyball, Earth Toss, or Earth Spin. I would like, however, to merely hold it in my arms as I would hold a grandchild, loving and protecting what it represents, on behalf not only of myself but of future generations, and on behalf of the God who so fiercely loves it.

Ponder and Pray

Preparation: Pick up a current newspaper or news magazine. Close your eyes, quiet down and become aware of God's presence with you. Then picture the earth from outer space. Think of the words of the astronauts who described its fragility and beauty, "where all the good stuff is." Think of the view of the earth–"the threshing-floor that makes us all so fierce"–as described by Dante. Imagine how God must look upon the earth.

Intercession: Now open your eyes and let your glance fall on the headlines. Choose an article that describes places far away where there is conflict or suffering. Does the situation come alive when you look at the earth this way? Does human suffering become less abstract and more real? Hold this situation before God as urgently as you would if the suffering occurred in your own home or neighborhood.

If you read the news on your computer, do a similar preparation beforehand (quieting down, closing your eyes, picturing the earth as God sees it), then choose a situation on the screen that especially engages you and hold it before God.

If you are accustomed to watching the news on television, quiet down after you have watched the news and turned off the TV. What particular event in the broadcast draws you to pray about the people involved?

8. EMBODIED

Do you not know that your body is a temple of the Holy Spirit within you, which you have from God, and that you are not your own? For you were bought with a price; therefore glorify God in your body.

—1 Corinthians 6:19-20

Just as viewing our blue-and-white earth from afar helps us to gain perspective, so moving in the other direction–into our bodies themselves–can give us insights about our relationship with nature and with God.

The husband-and-wife design team, Charles and Ray Eames (perhaps most known for their "Eames chairs"), created a short film in 1977 entitled *Powers of Ten*.[16] It begins with a photograph of an area one meter square, taken from one meter away, of a couple relaxing after a picnic on the shore of Lake Michigan in Chicago. The camera then moves away by powers of ten. When it is ten meters away, we see the wide grassy lawn on the lakefront; then we pull back to see the shoreline and the lake. Soon we look down and see the entire Great Lakes region, but are not able to dwell on the sight, for the camera keeps moving, until at ten to the seventh power–100,000,000 meters–we see the "Earth Ball"! The Eameses continue the cosmic journey: past the sun, beyond our solar system, through the Milky Way, out of our galaxy, and finally reach ten to the twenty-fourth power, as we rest in the great emptiness of the limits of our vision in outer space.

Now the camera reverses its journey, as if we were falling rapidly through space toward our planet. We eventually zero in on Chicago, then on the couple on the picnic blanket, and finally focus on the right hand of the man, who is asleep. Now the camera goes inward, past the surface of the hand, entering the skin at ten to the minus-second power. Into the blood vessels we go, into a white cell and its nucleus. We catch a glimpse of the beautiful double-helix that contains our DNA, burrow into the atoms, and move into the electrons in their shimmering quantum motion. We finally come to rest inside a single proton, the edge of current knowledge in 1977.

As we reflect on our relationship with the "Earth Ball" which is our home, this intimate perspective, also, is useful. The interior journey of the camera *reminds us* that *we are bodies*. Somehow or other, especially since the Enlightenment, with its emphasis on reason, and the Industrial Revolution, with its trust in technology, we have gotten decapitated. Or maybe it is the other way around: we have gotten de-bodied!

A Jules Feiffer cartoon from 1984 depicts a drawing of a man with his head floating in the air above his body. Next to the head is a description of its function: it thinks, talks, charms, worries, laughs, hurts. He is very proud of it! Besides the drawing of the body, however, the description is not as glowing: he thinks it is funny looking, is prone to malfunction, and looks best in winter clothes. The decapitated man has as little to do with his body as possible. However, it does have a purpose: "Lucky for my body that I need it to chauffeur my head around. Otherwise–out it would go!"

When we see the images on television or in magazines, it may seem to us that there is too *much* emphasis on the body in our culture rather than too little. But look more closely: the focus is usually on the body's outward appearance. Seductive ads for chic clothing and miracle cosmetics feature models who are often abnormally thin, and usually young and white. These images are intended to breed dissatisfaction with ourselves, as we begin to question our self-worth: "That is how I am supposed to look, too. Maybe I can look like that if I buy the product these beautiful people are using or wearing."

My favorite image to counteract this cultural emphasis on outward appearance is the apostle Paul's idea of our bodies as "temples of the Spirit." "Do you not know that your body is a temple of the Holy Spirit within you, which you have from God...?" We do not just *have* bodies, to be dressed and groomed like the Barbies or Kens that we might wish to resemble. We *are* bodies, and these bodies are temples—places of worship! They have much in common with the English cathedrals my husband and I have visited over the years. Each one is unique, with its own architectural style and character. Each is beautiful, but its beauty does not depend only on its architecture and decoration. No indeed. Because these buildings have been places of worship for so long, the atmosphere reverberates with the prayers and pilgrimages of centuries. It is the spirit within that beckons us, not merely the structure of stone, wood, and glass, although due attention is paid to the structure–there are few ancient cathedrals today without scaffolding. Nevertheless, the obvious signs of age, if they are not dangerous, are never erased. No one would think, for example, of smoothing out the photogenic steps to the chapter house of Wells Cathedral, worn smooth by centuries of footsteps. These places have character, provided by all the life that has happened within them. This is good news, especially, as we begin to notice our own marks of aging!

Our relationship to our bodies is very often similar to our relationship to the natural world. We sometimes pay scant attention to them, nor do we appreciate them. Do we know that we are bodies, filled with God's *ruach*: the gift of life-breath? Do we know that we are deeply a part of nature, not *apart from* nature? Do we know that our bodies are utterly dependent on the environment around us: that we would die without air, or water, or food? Perhaps a first step in looking at the subject of environmental ethics–before committing ourselves to recycling our garbage, composting our weeds, buying a fuel-efficient car, or contacting our political leaders about global warming–is to really notice our own bit of nature: that part that begins with the soles of our feet and ends at the top of our scalp. We can learn to be good stewards of the health of our bodies, and at the same time tend to the life within it, by filling our own inner space with the constant and joyful renewing of our relationship with our God.

We are not just a head being chauffeured around by our body. We are all of one piece, we "temples." We are feet that tread the earth, a digestive tract that processes earth's bounty. We are lungs that receive earth's oxygen and a circulatory system that courses throughout in order to carry that life-force everywhere within us. We are a heart that both functions mechanically and (metaphorically) feels passionately. We are a brain, a "mission control" that regulates it all, yet also receives the body's messages to the extent that some consider the body to be a part of the brain. Physically, we are a miraculous creation. *Holy* even.

To know that we are holy, transparent to God and given our very being by God, helps lead us to the next step: *everything else on earth* is holy, too.

Ponder and Pray

The creation story in Genesis 2 is a rich source of meditation. It presents a dramatic image of the human being as a creature of earth filled with God's gift of life. The Hebrew even embodies a play upon words: God molds *adamah,* or earth, breathes *ruach* (life-breath) into it, and it becomes *adam*–literally, an *earthling!* This word-picture of the human condition is yet another way of expressing the idea that we are "temples of the Spirit."

In this prayer exercise, your body itself participates in

the meditation.

Standing, or sitting in a chair, notice your weight. You have weight because of earth's gravity, pulling you like a magnet. Gravity is a physical reminder of our identity as *adams*–earthlings. We live here, on planet Earth. It is our *oikos*–our home. Take some time to notice this sensation of gravity, and what it signifies.

Now imagine the top of your head reaching for the sky as if it were being pulled upward by an invisible string. Relax your shoulders. Inhale, and welcome your breath, as a sign of the spirit or *ruach* of God. Allow your abdomen to expand as you breathe, then the rib cage–front, sides, and back. Picture the breath bringing to life into every cell of your body, from what is visible to the naked eye to the electrons in their shimmering quantum motion and the protons at the center of it all. Take some time to notice your breathing, and to feel the life it brings.

Thank God for your body, the temple in which you dwell during your life on this earth.

CONCERN

Answer me when I call, O God, defender of my cause;
you set me free when I am hard-pressed;
have mercy on me and hear my prayer.

Many are saying,
"Oh, that we might see better times!"
Lift up the light of your countenance upon us, O God.

—Psalm 4: 1, 6, The Saint Helena Psalter

We all know that a relationship grounded in love has the capacity to give us pain. Caring and compassion cause us to become vulnerable: hence both love's blessing and love's danger. When we love God's creation, we cannot help but mourn nature's losses. When we recognize that we are implicated merely because we live in a society that has too long ignored the well-being of the natural world, we can become burdened with guilt. But God calls us to cast off the burden of guilt and to move forward. We take our sorrow and our repentance before God, ask forgiveness, and seek to lead a new life. We do this both as individuals and as communities. And, indeed, like good compost, our sorrows and repentance can be transformed into new life for ourselves and for the world in which we live.

1. The Vine

The world is charged with the grandeur of God.
It will flame out, like shining from shook foil;
It gathers to a greatness, like the ooze of oil
Crushed. Why do men then now not reck his rod?
Generations have trod, have trod, have trod;
And all is seared with trade; bleared, smeared with toil;
And wears man's smudge and shares man's smell; the soil
Is bare now, nor can foot feel, being shod.

And for all this, nature is never spent;
There lives the dearest freshness deep down things;
And though the last lights off the black West went
O, morning, at the brown brink eastward, springs–
Because the Holy Ghost over the bent
World broods with warm breast and with ah! bright wings.[17]

—Gerard Manley Hopkins

My room in the house where I grew up was a magical place tucked under the eaves. Of the two windows, one had a view of my favorite climbing tree, a maple with strong branches at the top which served as a perch when I wanted to read, eat an apple, or simply day-dream. The view out of the other window was almost entirely obscured during the growing season by a bittersweet vine, planted either by my parents a decade before, or by a passing bird who had perched on the windowsill soon thereafter. Now the vine was a bird haven. They gathered in the luxuriance of its foliage for shelter from the heat of summer; they devoured its berries in the autumn, and in the winter it became a useful place to perch while cracking open the seeds from the feeder in the back yard.

The spring I was in third grade, my parents decided to have the house painted. They never thought to tell me about the impact it might make on my view. One day, I came home from school, and the vine was gone. Gone. I shut myself in my room, wept, and finally sought solace by writing a poem.

Oh that I wish that my vine was there,
But it isn't any more.
To hear the little birdies sing
Was the thing that I adore.

Not great poetry. But my mother later told me that when she found it on my desk the next morning after I'd gone to school, she was the one who had sobbed.

It was my first experience of environmental loss.

I have known human losses since then: my grandparents, my parents, and, ever increasingly, friends and family of my own generation. But now, I find that I mourn also for the non-human losses which are more and more part of today's headlines.

I discover grief welling up when I read about the last members of an endangered species, mountain valleys threatened by a new dam, or a melting icecap. I want to cover my eyes when we drive east on a route through coal-mining country and pass scenery desecrated by strip mining, or when I see from the window of an airplane that even uglier method of coal mining called mountain-top removal. Even the sound of a chain saw wielded by a local tree company makes me flinch; although the tree being felled is probably dead anyway, it had, in its decay, provided habitat for some lovely creatures.

Why this pain? It is, simply, because I care. My childhood laid the foundation for the pleasure I find, not only in my love for other human beings, but in my love for the natural world. If I hadn't cared for my grandparents or parents or friends, I would not have grieved when they died–and the same is true for the bittersweet vine, the icecap, and the mountains.

What should I do with this grief? What would you do with *yours?*

What I did was twofold: I began to educate myself, and I began to put my love into action. My caring and my sorrow have become, in short, a source of energy.

Some time ago, because I wanted to engage others in this exploration, I invited people in a large city parish to join me in a discussion group about the environment. The meetings very soon became gripe sessions, leaving us heavy-hearted with despair. I learned that the grief born from caring must bear fruit in action, for our own good as well as for the world's. Reasons for grief are all too well documented by scientists, and are summarized each year in Worldwatch Institute's *The State of the World.* I first read an issue of

The State of the World some twelve years ago, and learned, to my dismay, that some of that year's accelerating trends caused by human civilization: among them, "freshwater ecosystem deterioration, the emergence of new deadly diseases and the re-emergence of diseases once thought to have been conquered, the loss of topsoil, and the increasing number of pests resistant to pesticides."[18] And things have gone from bad to worse. After years of silence from the media, the environment is finally making the headlines. This morning, there popped up on my computer screen some bad news about the oceans. A map had just been released at the annual meeting of the American Association for the Advancement of Science that indicated that every single spot in the oceans has been affected by at least one human activity, and that damage includes reductions in fish and sea animals as well as severe threats to the existence of coral reefs, seagrass beds, mangroves, and rocky reefs.

How could I respond to such complex and vast problems? I wanted to. After all, I had graduated from a college that proclaims in its marketing material: "Think one person can change the world? So do we."

In this new world situation, above all, we need to learn from those people who know the most about how the world works: ecologists. Their field is the study of our *oikos*: in other words, good-housekeeping for our earthly home. We can't learn how to "change the world" only by reading the Bible or walking in the woods, although both of these activities might well motivate us to begin. At first, I had sought books with brave titles like *A Thousand Ways to Save the World or The Consumer's Guide to Planet Repair*. When we moved to Oberlin, with its opportunities to attend college classes, I enrolled in a class entitled "Environment and Society." As I sat in that classroom, I heard new language that I perceived as deeply theological. What I was hearing substantiated my growing belief that we needed to think differently about our place in the world. My ethics had already begun to change to include much more than what I had been taught in church. In a subsequent course on Environmental Ethics, taught (appropriately) by a Professor Care, I continued to lay the philosophical foundations for a broader, deeper, and more far-reaching moral code.

Fr. James Huntington, the founder of the Order of the Holy Cross, wrote, in his Rule for the monastic order, "Love must act as fire must burn."

Love must act. Love unexpressed in action can paralyze us with sorrow when what we love is threatened. When we are able to act, the energy of grief propels us forward in our work towards the healing of the world, and that work contributes to our own healing.

The great naturalist John Muir is called the "Father of our National Parks." To greatly oversimplify the tale, it was a single decision on his part that led to that title: in 1903, he asked President Theodore Roosevelt to go camping with him in Yosemite. When Roosevelt had assumed office in 1901, half of the nation's timberlands had already been cut down, and special interests were gathering forces to lay waste to huge tracts of pristine wilderness. As the two men hiked, Roosevelt's eyes were opened by the beauty he saw, and thanks to him, the first five national parks were created, along with other conservation projects such as national forests, bird refuges, and game preserves. Think one person (like John Muir, or like you) can change the world? We'll explore the possibilities as we continue this journey together. Love must act, as fire must burn.

Ponder and Pray

It is difficult to deal with the pain of environmental loss. We all contribute to its causes, simply by living in an affluent society in the twenty-first century. Sit quietly with your feelings. Then, on behalf of humanity as a whole, and with a sense of your unwitting involvement in nature's predicament, offer to God this prayer of contrition:

We have forgotten who we are.

We have forgotten who we are
We have alienated ourselves from the unfolding of the cosmos
We have become estranged from the movements of the earth
We have turned our backs on the cycles of life.

We have forgotten who we are

We have sought only our own security
We have exploited simply for our own ends

We have distorted our knowledge
We have abused our power

We have forgotten who we are

Now the land is barren
And the waters are poisoned
And the air is polluted

We have forgotten who we are

Now the forests are dying
And the creatures are disappearing
And humans are despairing

We have forgotten who we are

We ask forgiveness
We ask for the gift of remembering
We ask for the strength to change.

We have forgotten who we are.

—*U. N. Environmental Sabbath Program* [19]

The wisdom of the spiritual tradition guides us to seek
what is called "amendment of life" after a prayer of contrition. Rather than wallowing in guilt, we are advised to
accept the invitation to change. Pray the following prayer
now, on behalf of yourself and of all humanity.

O Holy God,
May we love and respect all your creation,
all the earth and every grain of sand in it.
May we love every leaf,
every ray of your light.
May we love the animals:
you have given them the rudiments of thought and joy untroubled.
Let us not trouble them;
let us not harass them,
let us not deprive them of their happiness,
let us not work against your intentions.
For we acknowledge that to withhold any measure of love from
anything in the universe
is to withhold that same measure from you.

—Fyodor Dostoyevsky[20]

2. The Snows of Kilimanjaro

Grandfather,
Look at our brokenness.

We know that in all creation
Only the human family
Has strayed from the Sacred Way.

We know that we are the ones
Who are divided
And we are the ones
Who must come back together
To walk in the Sacred Way.

Grandfather,
Sacred One,
Teach us love, compassion, and honor
That we may heal the earth
And heal each other.

—Ojibway Prayer [21]

On a certain Monday a few years ago, the breaking news was that the icecap of Mount Kilimanjaro had melted. I did not overlook the irony that on Friday of that week I had entered a hospital for removal of part of my left breast. Everyone agreed that I was an unlikely candidate for the disease. There was no family history of breast cancer, and I had eaten carefully and exercised vigorously all my life, had two pregnancies and breast-fed my children. Cancer was a startling and unwelcome surprise.

During the week that began with the announcement about Kilimanjaro's icecap and ended with my surgery, a conviction began to grow that these were not disconnected events. Although I was not nearly as well endowed as the African mountain, I suspected that both our losses had environmental degradation at their root. I remembered what I had scribbled in my environmental studies notebook: "Human society is embedded in nature. When we abuse nature, we are compromising our own well-being as well."

Certainly the disappearance of the icecap was due to abuse of nature. Since 1912, the mountain's ice fields, described by Ernest Hemingway as "wide as all the world, great, high, and unbelievably white in the sun," have lost eighty-two percent of their ice. It is now predicted that these great glaciers may be gone entirely by 2020. Researchers are scrambling to collect core samples of Kilimanjaro's glaciers, in order to store them in freezers until more sophisticated technology is available with which to study them. It has even been suggested that it might be possible to cover the mountain's ice cap with a kind of prosthesis: a bright white cover–inspired by those used in England to protect cricket fields from the elements–to serve as a membrane to seal the glaciers, prevent evaporation, and reflect solar radiation. Scientists attribute the melting of Kilimanjaro's icecap both to global warming and to local human activities, such as the clearing of forests by farmers and the setting of fires by honey collectors trying to smoke bees out of their hives. The combined impact of both had created a burden that was more than the mountain could bear.

As I read about the research on cancer, I discovered that I also had been bearing a burden. Studies by the Centers for Disease Control and Prevention have shown that Americans of all ages carry what is called a "body burden" of at least one hundred sixteen synthetic chemicals, some of which have been banned for more than two decades because of their toxicity. I tried to picture what toxins might have become part of my own body burden. Could they have resided in insecticides that had been intended to rid our back yards of mosquitoes but also wiped out for a few decades the fireflies who once provided our favorite entertainment on a summer's night, as we tried to catch them, glass jars at the ready? (We released them before our bedtime.) Could my skin have absorbed the toxins through cosmetics marketed without proper screening for their health impact, or meat from animals whose food was laced with hormones? Could I have breathed the toxins streaming into the family car on long trips in mid-summer before automobile air conditioning was routine? Did the sharp odor from the backing of the wall-to-wall carpet we bought for our first house indicate we were inhaling something poisonous? I had believed the world was safe, but now I knew it was not. This disease was my legacy from a society that has been ignorant over the years, or, worse, has chosen to prioritize profit rather than safety. I had become a victim of runaway industrial technology and the market: to put it bluntly, human greed.

It has always puzzled me that the appeals I have received over the years from most cancer organizations emphasize "finding a cure." Although I am the last person who would suggest that researchers abandon that goal, I myself would prefer donating to an organization whose goal is to find and publicize the causes of this epidemic. I would like them to identify what toxins were in the food I ate or the water I drank, what poisons were in the air I breathed, what radiation bombarded me–so that a single healthy cell went haywire. Grateful as I am for the medical skill that detected a very early cancer and then provided the cure, to neglect what scientists call the "etiology" of a disease sounds like a case of what my grandmother (who grew up in the days before automobiles and garages) called "locking the barn door after the horse is stolen."

The snow will never sculpt the top of Kilimanjaro again, nor will my missing few ounces of flesh be restored as good as new. I cannot claim that the change in my own silhouette, which was never voluptuous in the first place, will have the impact of Kilimanjaro's loss of form. In the case of the mountain, it is predicted that visits by tourists and climbers will begin to dwindle, and that the local economy will be undermined, melted along with the snow.

In the local cancer center, a pamphlet declares that cancer is a disease not only of the body, but of mind and spirit as well. Support groups, yoga, reiki, and massage are provided.

But what comforts me most – beyond yoga, or massage, or even prayer–is this: *the cancer was not my fault.* Instead, my disease was in the nature of an automobile accident caused by a careless driver. In this case, the "driver" is a society that neglects the "precautionary principle," which dictates that manufacturers first ascertain, beyond the shadow of a doubt, that a product will do no harm before it is put on the market. Our elected officials, who are obligated to serve the public interest by protecting us from accumulating these un-asked-for body burdens, should insist on it, and we should insist that they do so.

Some cancers find their causes elsewhere, in lifestyle is-sues like smoking or diet, or in the genes we happen to in-herit—and I know that our susceptibility increases with age. But in the end, I have decided to claim Kilimanjaro as a partner in loss, and take some comfort in acknowledging my solidarity with her. We are two creations of God, blem-ished now because of something totally outside of ourselves. I, at least, can find solace in trying to work towards prevent-ing its happening to others. The mountain and I have been connected through our vulnerability. We are soul-sisters.

Ponder and Pray

Read the story of the healing of blind Bartimaeus:

> As Jesus and his disciples and a large crowd were leaving Jericho, Bartimaeus son of Timaeus, a blind beggar, was sitting by the roadside. When he heard that it was Jesus of

Nazareth, he began to shout out and say, "Jesus, Son of David, have mercy on me!" Many sternly ordered him to be quiet, but he cried out even more loudly, "Son of David, have mercy on me!" Jesus stood still and said, "Call him here." And they called the blind man, saying to him, "Take heart; get up, he is calling you." So throwing off his cloak, he sprang up and came to Jesus. Then Jesus said to him, "What do you want me to do for you?" The blind man said to him, "My teacher, let me see again." Jesus said to him, "Go; your faith has made you well" Immediately he regained his sight and followed him on the way. (Mark 10: 46b-52)

This story can be understood on many levels, one of which might be as a pattern of how we and our planet can seek health and wholeness. Read it slowly, and ask yourself these questions:

What feelings might have caused Bartimaeus to cry out so vehemently and persistently?

Why might people have rebuked him for his persistence?

Why do you think that Jesus stopped?

Why did Jesus, who must have observed that Bartimaeus was blind, ask him what he wanted?

What did Jesus mean when he said that Bartimaeus' "faith" had made him well?

Why did Bartimaeus now follow Jesus on his way?

What does this story mean to us, in terms of our need to speak out persistently, to accept God's healing of ourselves, and then to become a healing presence in the world by "following the Healer"?

3. Hard-wired

O shame to us who rest content, while lust and greed for gain in street and shop and tenement wring gold from human pain, and bitter lips in blind despair cry, "Christ hath died in vain."

Give us, O God, the strength to build the city that hath stood too long a dream, whose laws are love, whose crown is ser-vanthood, and where the sun that shineth is God's grace for human good.

—*Walter Russell Bowie, 1882-1969* [22]

"Don't just sit there. Do something!" Confronted with the loss of those things we hold dear–forests, snow-capped mountains, bittersweet vines, clean water, clear air–we have often wanted to cry out these words in protest. Why did it taken so long for the world to pay attention? Why the leth-argy exhibited by everyone from our national leaders to cor-porations, communities, and even churches, where people know by heart the lines in Genesis, "God saw everything that he had made, and indeed, it was very good."? Why have we not done all that is humanly possible to preserve the world God gave us for our earthly home?

David Orr, the noted professor who taught "Environ-ment and Society," hit the nail on the head one day in class. "We human beings are hard-wired for crisis. We are not good at responding to long-term threats."

Embedded in our genetic makeup is the life experience of our distant ancestors, who did indeed need to focus their concern on immediate threats, rather than long-term ones: the tiger hiding in the underbrush, or the human foe about to strike. If they *did* something, they lived to produce progeny. If they just sat there, they might have been devoured or murdered. The "fight or flight response" is our physiological reminder of this legacy. When we get a summons from an irate boss or lose track of a toddler in the supermarket, adrenalin floods our body, causing our pulse and breathing to quicken and our muscles to contract. Our bodies become ready for action.

Historically, long-term threats such as global warming or world poverty have not made us go into the "fight or flight" mode. Until recently, there has not been an obvious trigger for action produced by issues, like climate change, that most threaten us today. Instead, it is the dramatic disaster, whether natural or manmade, that catches our attention. A good example is the way people worldwide responded to the tsunami in the Indian Ocean early in 2005 or to Hurricane Katrina later that year. I know a parish that had labored long and hard to raise money for its one-hundred-fiftieth anniversary celebration at about the time the tsunami roiled the Indian Ocean. The Sunday after the tragedy, the vestry met briefly after church and soon reported that they had voted to give all the money to relief efforts. Less than nine months later, after Katrina had pounded the Gulf Coast, a retired priest in his eighties, from the same parish, simply got in his car a couple of days later and drove down to Louisiana to report for pastoral duty in a relief center.

But there are ongoing "tsunamis" and "hurricanes" that create even more devastating loss of life every single day of the year; it's just that they don't tend to set our hearts to racing. Their names are Poverty, Famine, and War. These causes of chronic suffering do not often appear on the evening news. The situation is as if our body were becoming more and more stooped with progressive osteoporosis, ignored by us until a broken hip finally lands us in the hospital emergency room.

It is admirable, of course, to help when there is a catastrophe, and tsunamis, earthquakes, hurricanes, and acts of terrorism have inspired much self-sacrifice. Long-term challenges like climate change may not stir us up in the same way, but they have the potential to change life on this earth to a much more dangerous extent than any natural disaster has yet done. Elizabeth Kolbert writes, in a series of essays in *The New Yorker*:

> Just a few degrees more and the earth will be hotter than it has been at any time since our species evolved....As the effects of global warming become more and more apparent, will we react by finally fashioning a global response? Or will we retreat into ever narrower and more destructive forms of self-interest? It may seem impossible to imagine that a technologically advanced society could choose, in essence, to destroy itself, but that is what we are now in the process of doing.[23]

How does our faith help us in these times? Some would say that earthly well-being does not matter, because we are destined for heavenly bliss. But I would disagree. I believe that God means us to care for this lovely planet, and that God is calling us to look clearly and courageously at its plight. Climate change will be most devastating for those already in greatest need–the poor, the hungry, the dispossessed–those whom Jesus said were most beloved of God.

I believe that our faith calls us to listen: to listen to the information that science is giving us. Such listening is a form of holy obedience–a word that finds its root in the Latin *obedire*: "to give ear, to hearken, to obey." God wants us to hear the truth, and then act on it, to the best of our abilities.

Will we succeed in preventing a potential catastrophe? We do not know. But it has been said, "It is not necessary to succeed; it is only necessary to be faithful." And faithfulness might lead to success. Imagine what would happen if people all over the globe looked at the truth and then responded with passion and creativity? God the Creator has given us free will, and thus cannot singlehandedly save us from our predicament. But God the healer is calling us to join in the healing, while there is yet time to do so.

Ponder and Pray

This was a painful chapter to write. How did you feel as you were reading it? Do you have any examples from your life in which discomfort has been a symptom of God's calling you to something new?

In a clergy wellness program I know, one of the conference leaders projects on a screen an image: a large square, partitioned into quarters. Above the left section of the top is the word "urgent" and above the right section is "not urgent." To the left of the two side sections are the words "important" and "not too important." Each quarter represents a different combination of these categories, and participants are invited think of activities that fit each one. An example of "not urgent/not important" might be rearranging the paperclips and pencils in a desk drawer, while "urgent/not important" might be agreeing to run to the wine shop because the altar guild has run out of communion wine. Making a hospital visit to a parishioner who has just been in an automobile accident would fall into the category of "urgent/important," while "not urgent/important" could be any number of things that are absolutely essential to one's own and the church's well-being, such as making time for prayer, writing the book you've had on the back burner for years, or taking time for your family.

Can you think of examples from your own life of each of these categories? Do you notice how easy it is to postpone those activities that fall under "important/not urgent"?

This personal difficulty is mirrored in our society. I have already provided two examples: global warming and world poverty. What are some other examples?

4. Untapped

In the year that King Uzziah died, I saw the Lord sitting on
a throne, high and lofty; and the hem of his robe filled the
temple. Seraphs were in attendance above him; each had six
wings: with two they covered their faces, and with two they
covered their feet, and with two they flew. And one called to
another and said: "Holy, holy, holy is the Lord of hosts; the
whole earth is full of his glory." And the pivots on the thresh-
olds shook at the voices of those who called, and the house
filled with smoke. And I said, "Woe is me! I am lost, for I am
a man of unclean lips, and I live among a people of unclean
lips; yet my eyes have seen the King, the Lord of hosts!"

Then one of the seraphs flew to me, holding a live coal that
had been taken from the altar with a pair of tongs. The
seraph touched my mouth with it and said: "Now that this
has touched your lips, your guilt has departed and your sin
is blotted out." Then I heard the voice of the Lord saying,
"Whom shall I send, and who will go for us?" And I said,
"Here am I; send me!"

—Isaiah 6: 1-9

We used to spend our summers in a yellow clapboard
house over two centuries old, nestled in the woodland of
central New Hampshire. It was owned by Rosemary, a business colleague of my father, who was able to use it only one
month of the year. It had been her family's tradition to share

the home with others. One spring when we were pondering how to spend our first summer as the financially challenged parents of a newborn, we received a letter inviting us to vacation in her little house. She included captivating photos, and we accepted the invitation by return mail.

As our family grew, and Rosemary also began to spend more time there, she began to notice that occasionally her well water was in short supply. After a summer during which we all had to take sponge baths rather than use her capacious bathtub and, weather permitting, use the woods for an outhouse, she called upon a no-nonsense New Hampshire native by the name of Roy Grace, a skilled carpenter and handyman, who also happened to be a dowser. Rosemary accompanied him as he walked around the meadow behind the house, holding the forked branch of an apple tree. She later told us that suddenly the branch seemed to be forcibly jerked downwards. "There's your water!"

Roy was able to estimate how deep the well would have to be dug and how abundant its flow of water would be. I decided that his last name was no accident.

Where is such "water" for this suffering planet, thirsty for the healing resource that is human intelligence, wisdom, and creativity? Is it lying hidden and untapped, like the water source that was to feed Rosemary's new well?

The resource is, I believe, the power of God working through each of *us*–the readers of this book, the people in the pews and the sanctuaries of our places of worship, laity and the ordained, as well as all the other spiritual seekers who desire to leave the world around them better than they found it. I hope it does not seem ridiculous that I can even picture God seeking us with a dousing stick called Grace. When it hovers above hearts that are open, we are drawn like water to Roy Grace's apple branch, until we respond, like Isaiah, "Here am I am. Send me."

There is a wonderful image in the final chapter of the Revelation to John, the last book of the Bible. The river of the water of life, "bright as crystal," flows from God's throne through the middle of the street of a city. (Rev. 22:1) We all can be part of that healing river, bordered with fruit-bearing trees–and the more of us there are, the more life-giving that water becomes. It is quite clear by now that we cannot depend only on those in high places to do the work. Instead, it is up to each of us to contribute our gifts of intellect, heart, and action to the river of life.

But it may take some training for us to do this effectively.

We need, first, to go beyond the stumbling blocks we encountered in the previous chapters: apathy, fear, pain, the desire to avoid inconvenience, or the paralysis that results from feeling overwhelmed. We need to be brave enough to leave behind our comfortable insularity, and to claim our kinship with the entire web of life. We need to be wise and humble enough to let ourselves be educated by those scientists who devote their lives to understanding the natural world, and we need to be guided by God's grace. The words "spiritual formation" and "education" come to mind.

Those of us who walk the Christian way can find that our spiritual ancestors provide very good company—those saints, mystics, and theologians of the church who celebrated the holiness of the natural world. We can learn from other world religions and from indigenous peoples. We also can consider the moral codes that amplify the Great Commandment to love God and our neighbor, and use their guidelines as a structure for broadening our ethical frame of reference. We have words—sacrament, sin, freedom, love, transformation—that will serve well as we undertake this task.

We have, above all, the will to do good, rather than to do harm. We can ignore the siren song of our culture, for we know that satisfaction does not lie in power and possessions. Instead we follow another voice:

"Blessed are the meek...Blessed are the merciful...Blessed are the peacemakers....You are the salt of the earth....You are the light of the world...Love your enemies...Do not store up for yourselves treasures on earth, where moth and rust consume and where thieves break in and steal; but store up for yourselves treasures in heaven...for where your treasure is, there your hearts will be also....Truly I tell you, just as you did it to one of the least of these who are members of my family, you did it to me."

That voice calls to us to allow God's healing to flow through us to the world around us. What better way could there be to describe the abundant life for which we all long?

Ponder and Pray

Read once again the "call of Isaiah," the passage with which this chapter began. Although Isaiah describes the event in outward, visual terms, do you think that he was describing an *inner* sense of being called by God to give his life to God's service, as well?

The writer Frederick Beuchner describes vocation (based on the Latin word for "call") as the "place where your deep gladness and the world's deep hunger meet."[24] Have you ever experienced such a call? When? (It need not be "religious" in the narrow sense of that word: people as diverse as musicians, doctors, tree surgeons, carpenters, and community activists describe their occupations as vocations.)

How does maintaining the health and beauty of our environment contribute to your "deep gladness"?

In what ways has the "deep hunger" of the planet called to you?

Do you understand your response to this "deep hunger" as being *Grounded in Love?*

5. The Good Friday Walk

Oh love, how deep, how broad, how high,
how passing thought and fantasy,
that God, the Son of God, should take
our mortal form for mortals' sake....

For us to wicked hands betrayed,
scourged, mocked, in purple robe arrayed,
he bore the shameful cross and death;
for us gave up his dying breath....

All glory to our Lord and God
for love so deep, so high, so broad;
the Trinity whom we adore
for ever and for evermore.

—*The Hymnal 1982 (Latin, fifteenth century; tr. Benjamin Webb)*

Good Friday happened to fall one year on a spring day that was pure gift in northern Ohio–alive with birdsong, the serenades of young frogs, and the warmth of the long-awaited sun. As I knelt taking my turn at the prayer vigil inside our small parish church, I had the distinct intuition that I had to respond to the Creator of all this beauty by quietly slipping outside to continue my observation of this solemn day in the open air. When my time was up, I closed the heavy wooden door behind me and headed for the nature preserve on the western edge of town.

On the way, I passed a tall sweetgum tree. I have always enjoyed the staccato texture of sweetgum pods, and, at this time of year, their spiked spheres lie at the base of their mother trees like fallen blossoms. I leaned down and picked up three of them. Their texture initiated a surprising sequence of thoughts: "How strange that I picked up three—a Trinity. They feel like a crown of thorns, on the day we remember the crucifixion of Jesus, the second person of the Trinity. Could it be that *all three persons* of the Trinity are 'crucified' through sin?"

Could we be crucifying the Creator, I mused? When our lives and actions become death-dealing to God's earth, does our Creator suffer? Could this time be a kind of twenty-first-century Calvary? It was a stark vision, from which I would have liked to avert my gaze. I would have preferred to be Dame Julian of Norwich, holding the small orb of a hazelnut in her hand and seeing in it all that God made and loved. Instead, with the sweetgum pod prickling my palm, I saw how human beings, with their infinite capacity for sin as well as for goodness, can crown with thorns God's beloved creation

Pocketing the sweetgum pods, I continued walking down the lane that leads into the nature preserve, where a clay dike contains the water of an old reservoir and a short trail loops through swamp and woodland. The leaves of trout lilies were poking through the forest humus, signaling the arrival of Spring. But the sweetgum pods kept irritating me, like a hair shirt, whenever I put my hand in my pocket. Why couldn't I just enjoy nature and focus on God, without such negative thoughts?

At the end of the path, a flight of wooden steps took me up to the reservoir, and I sat on a bench looking over the water. Way out in the middle was a lone bird low in the water—a loon. The loon reminded me of a poem someone gave me once, about a duck resting in the infinity of the ocean, trusting the water and the waves to support her. The poem concludes, "the duck has religion." The loon was resting in its own infinity, too—resting in the reservoir, doing what a loon ought to do. The loon had religion.

How can we rest in infinity, I wondered? How can human beings become as attuned to our earthly home as the duck and the loon? How can we "have religion," in this most authentic sense? How can we fit in with God's design for the world? And why is it that so many good people, who wouldn't ever dream of lying or stealing or committing adultery, don't even think about any of this?

Maybe, I thought, it is time for some new ways of thinking—and for some ethical guidelines based on resting in, and caring for, rather than crucifying, the earthly creation of God. And perhaps today, Good Friday, is a perfect day for me to begin to do this.

When I was a fervent teenager, I was very fond of a small black book called *St. Augustine's Prayer Book*. The book is still on my shelf, the pages crinkled and the cover loose because of an episode long ago when it accidentally went through an entire laundry cycle with my family's clothes.

But no amount of detergent, hot water, or agitation, could wash away the wisdom I found there in my youth, especially in the section called "Self-Examination," which provided me with a regular opportunity to measure my behavior against the tenets of the Ten Commandments. Under each commandment were printed questions suggesting possible transgressions–some of which I did not yet, in my naiveté, even understand.

While these old-fashioned pages sometimes make me smile now, the idea of self-examination is never out of date, not only on Good Friday but on all the days of the week of the entire year. Because the questions in my little black prayer book no longer suffice, we will need to interpret anew how we can love God with all our heart, and soul, and strength, and mind, and our neighbors as ourselves.

I like the inclusion of "mind" in the above, for contemporary Christians need to engage our minds in considering all the new ways in which we can respond to Jesus' call to love. In environmental studies classes, I heard new language that can give us guidance about how to love God and God's creation–more deeply, more broadly, and more passionately. This language poses some different questions from those in my battered *St. Augustine's Prayer Book,* but they will be useful guides to life in the twenty-first century. We'll soon consider what some of the guidelines might be.

Ponder and Pray

The author M. Scott Peck, in *The Road Less Traveled,*

defines love as the "will to extend one's self for the purpose of nurturing one's own or another's spiritual growth."[25] Peck's words can be a beginning for our reflection. They imply that love is an activity of the *will,* not merely a feeling of the "heart." But I would add to his definition: love is the will to extend one's self for the purpose of nurturing the well-being of oneself, someone else, or some*thing* else.

If we want to love someone, even ourselves, we have to find out what nurtures well-being. For example, loving myself does not give me free rein to indulge myself in eating a diet only of desserts. Rather, it means educating myself in healthy nutrition, then using my will to make informed choices. Loving my children does not mean smothering them by trying to live vicariously through them, but discovering their unique gifts and doing everything I can to help them claim and use their talents. Loving a tract of forest on our property means that we will not want to sell it to developers who will cut down all the trees, but will want to learn how best to help it flourish.

Now think an example of environmental degradation. What is the source of the damage? Lack of knowledge? Apathy? Greed? Does this example relate, or not relate, to human sin? Most of all, how does it relate, or not relate, to love?

What change of heart in human beings would help to heal that degradation? What actions might follow, for the purpose of nurturing well-being?

ETHICS

Let love be genuine; hate what is evil, hold fast to what is good; love one another with mutual affection; outdo one another in showing honor. Do not lag in zeal, be ardent in spirit, serve the Lord. Rejoice in hope, be patient in suffering, persevere in prayer. Contribute to the needs of the saints; extend hospitality to strangers. Bless those who persecute you; bless and do not curse them. Rejoice with those who rejoice, weep with those who weep. Live in harmony with one another; do not be haughty, but associate with the lowly; do not claim to be wiser than you are. Do not repay anyone evil for evil, but take thought for what is noble in the sight of all. If it is possible, so far as it depends on you, live peaceably with all.

—*Romans 12: 9-18*

Nurturing the new life we seek requires new knowledge, because we face issues unheard of in the times when our moral codes were first recorded. People of many faith traditions give us insights about how traditional ethics taught in churches, synagogues, mosques, and temples can be expanded to include our relationship to nature. All have one goal: to discover how love of God and neighbor can be embodied in ordinary daily life in this world. Thus, our moral decisions themselves, whether they concern how we vote, what we buy, how we treat one another, or what our attitude is toward a forest, a river, or an ocean, are grounded in love. In this section we will begin with a comparison of two different lifestyles, one the expression of a morality that includes the natural world, and one that does not. We will then hear some of the voices of today's faith communities, as they seek to frame a theology that will guide them in the endeavor to be good stewards of creation. Finally, we will discover how one particular ethical code, the Ten Commandments, formulated by a desert people over three thousand years ago, might serve as a series of guideposts to help us respond to today's particular call to love God and our neighbor.

1. Theo-Ecology

The idea that the laws that govern the world of nature and the laws which govern human society are interrelated is one of the universal elements of all the different religions, expressed in many different languages....If a mullah tells somebody in a mosque not to pollute the water, it will have a lot more effect than the government publishing an article about it in a newspaper in Cairo, Damascus or Tehran. The fact is that we all live on the globe within a web of life and an ecological system now being threatened with destruction through the manner in which we live.[26]

—*Seyyed Hossein Nasr*

There are two places I know well, where people gather in communities committed to serving the world around them.

In one place, containers are lined up outside the kitchen, marked "glass," "plastics," "metal," "cardboard," and "paper." A "free bin" is reserved for clothes no longer needed by community members, and under the kitchen sink are two pails labeled "compost" and "chickens." Much of the food is produced in the organic garden a few hundred feet away, and the buildings are made from local materials. An array of bicycles and a few cars, often shared, grace the parking lot. Our son Christopher lives in this place, in a well-insulated yurt powered by solar energy, which runs his computer, lights, and sound system. Publications from this community,[27] which is dedicated to environmental education, are printed on recycled paper or sent out via the internet. People come here to connect with the land and to learn how to be good stewards of nature.

In the second community, there are no recycling bins: paper, plastics, and metal are tossed in the garbage. The lights in the office blaze even when no one is there, and the air conditioning runs even on cool days. The perfect grass is maintained by a chemical lawn service. The office copying machine consumes vast amounts of virgin paper in its task of printing memos and bulletins, usually on one side of the page. The parking lot is crowded with gas-guzzling cars, in which people leave for home after drinking non-fair-traded coffee out of styrofoam cups. They gather in this place every week to worship God, the creator of the earth, where every so often they hear the great commandment: "You shall love the Lord your God with all your heart, and with all your soul, and with all your mind, and your neighbor as yourself."

Both communities are communities of good and well-meaning people. The first is an intentional environmental community in Oregon. The second is an imaginary place of worship, called whatever you wish to name it–perhaps St. Swithin's-in-the-Swamp! Fortunately, there are fewer examples of St. Swithin's these days, as people of faith are becoming more and more conscious of environmental stewardship. But we should not be harsh, should we discover a place that fits the description, for religious leaders generally have not had the advantage of the science curriculum most of our children are exposed to nowadays, with its emphasis on caring for the earth. All it might take to change St. Swithin's is a bit of education.

The good news is that every St. Swithin's has the capacity to change. Many years ago, I preached an Earth Day sermon in a downtown Manhattan church, in which I took note of the damage caused by the production and disposal of the tens of thousands of styrofoam cups from the thousands of coffee hours that Sunday throughout the nation. The next week, we drank from china!

For change to endure, we have to change the way we think. As I sat in my first environmental studies class, I heard some new language. Words like "sustainability," "ecological design," and "full-cost accounting" fill my student notebook. Like a child's wooden puzzle pieces scattered on the floor, then picked up and placed next to one another, they began to offer a design suggesting how human beings can best live in harmony with our earthly home. It dawned on me that this was a new way of describing God's call to love. Despite the fact that our professor respected the diversity of the student body by never mentioning God, I began to find myself coining a new word for what I was hearing: *Theo-ecology*. It shed new light on the Great Commandment, which has its source in the Hebrew Scriptures and was the core of Jesus' teachings: "Love the Lord your God with all your heart, with all your soul, with all your mind, and with all your strength....Love your neighbor as yourself." In his book, *The Universe is a Green Dragon*,[28] the physicist Brian

Swimme suggests that love, which he calls "allurement," is the force that makes the universe work. It occurs on the cosmic scale, in the form of gravity, which attracts galaxy to galaxy, as well as our bodies to the earth beneath our feet. Allurement also orchestrates our human world. We are "pulled toward" one another to become couples, families, and communities. We are drawn by the things we love to do, and thereby find our vocations in the world. We are seduced by the beauty of a Vermeer painting, the music of Bach, or the exquisite symmetry of an equation. When we take the time to fall under its spell, allurement beckons us towards ecstasy through immersion in the aliveness of the natural world. As Julian of Norwich wrote seven centuries ago, "Love was His meaning."

Love, however, is more than a "feeling of allurement." Like the gravitational force of the moon on the ocean, love *acts.* "Love must act as fire must burn." Loving our neighbor is not primarily a feeling. To love means to desire another's well-being.

Most of us have been taught since our early years about the ethics of loving our neighbor. I knew I wasn't supposed to hit my little brother, no matter how irritating his teasing became, although my ideal behavior was more often than not honored in the breach. I tried valiantly, and sometimes successfully, to refrain from joining in the gossip about the new girl in school. I knew I wasn't supposed to lie, cheat, or steal. But eventually, I realized that love was *not* just about not doing harm. It could also be about taking action–helping out in a soup kitchen or visiting a sick neighbor or elderly relative.

Our concept of love needs to continue to grow, in terms of time, space, and species. It needs to grow beyond our love of God and our human neighbors. For that, we need education, so that people of faith will begin to include in their ethical codes not only other human beings, but all of God's creation.

Ponder and Pray

If you attend a place of worship, how is it different from, or similar to, St. Swithin's-in-the-Swamp? How is your place of business different from, or similar to, St. Swithin's? How about your home?

How would each place compare to the environmental community I describe?

2. Commandments and Catechisms

The wolf shall live with the lamb,
* the leopard shall lie down with the kid,*
the calf and the lion and the fatling together,
* and a little child shall lead them.*
The cow and the bear shall graze,
* their young shall lie down together;*
* and the lion shall eat straw like the ox.*
The nursing child shall play over the hole of the asp,
* and the weaned child shall put its hand on the adder's den.*
They will not hurt or destroy on all my holy mountain;
for the earth will be full of the knowledge of the Lord
as the waters cover the sea.

—Isaiah 11:6-9

In first grade, I had a Sunday School teacher who taught through multi-media long before the days of videos, DVDs, or Power Point. She simply used a flannel board: an easel covered with wool flannel upon which she would stick cardboard cutouts backed with sandpaper. When she told the story of Moses and the Ten Commandments, she would walk a cardboard Moses up a cardboard Mount Sinai, magically produce the stone tablets of the law from behind her back, and then walk him down again to the waiting crowd of impatient cardboard Israelites. When it came to helping us memorize Bible verses, she sometimes lapsed into puns, such as when she would use a cutout drawing of a sailor's *knot* for the word "not," which we–being newly introduced to the written language–thought extremely funny.

Although we think of the Ten Commandments brought down from Sinai by an all-too-human Moses as *"nots,"* I think that maybe my Sunday School teacher was closer to the truth. We can understand them either as a set of rules about what not to do, or we can understand them as expressing our relationship with God and our neighbors–ways to tie the *knot* of harmonious community with both, if you will. The first four commandments are like a *midrash*, or commentary, on what it means to love God with all our heart, and soul, and mind, and strength, and the remaining six elaborate on the theme of loving our neighbor.

Where does our relationship with nature, that web of life to which we as human beings are so inextricably knotted, come in? The Hebrew nomads who brought the story of Moses and the Ten Commandments with them to the Promised Land, and those who finally recorded the text on scrolls, lived so lightly on the earth that the idea of commandments about caring for nature never occurred to them, unfortunately for us who live after the industrial revolution. It has been suggested that an "Eleventh Commandment" might be added—"Thou shalt not despoil the earth"—indicating that our behavior should not be molded by texts from a past era of human civilization alone. As our numbers increase, along with our capacity for doing harm, so must our understandings of the ethics which guides our lives.

People of all faith traditions are realizing this. I have tried to include the wisdom of other world religions in the quotations preceding each chapter, for the task ahead is a global one, and every voice needs to be heard. As for Christian denominations, a section in the *Greening Congregations Handbook,* published by Earth Ministry in 2002,[29] includes official statements about the environment from many sources. (Appendix references below are to this book.)

The Network for Environmental and Economic Responsibility of the United Church of Christ has issued this declaration:

> We believe that our planetary future is radically jeopardized by economic competition and growth unrestrained by a sense of limits about our place in the whole. Our love for our children and our children's children requires us to raise serious questions about the level and methods of production and the wasteful style of consumption in the United States and other affluent nations and people....We seek to cultivate attitudes of sacred covenanting among peoples and between humanity and the non-human creation. We call upon all members and instrumentalities of the United Church of Christ to display courageous leadership in:
>
> •modeling ecologically responsible lifestyles;
> •developing a communal spirituality able to connect persons creatively to the one, good creation of God; and
> •advocating for economic and technological change so that our earth has a green and sustainable future of just peace for all. (Appendix 39)

Quakers, who have often been at the forefront when it comes to social justice, write in a brochure produced by the Friends Committee on Unity with Nature:

> We have an obligation...to be responsible stewards of the earth, to restore its natural habitat where it has been damaged, and to maintain its vitality. Friends' historic testimonies on simplicity have long stressed that the quality of life does not depend upon immodest consumption. The urgency of the threat to the environment cannot be overstated. (Appendix 33)

The Presbyterians add their voice:

> ...Earth-keeping today means insisting on sustainability–the ongoing capacity of natural and social systems to thrive together–which requires human beings to practice wise, humble, responsible stewardship, after the model of servanthood that we have in Jesus. (Appendix 31)

As do the Roman Catholics:

> Today, the dramatic threat of ecological breakdown is teaching us the extent to which greed and selfishness–both individual and collective–are contrary to the order of creation, an order which is characterized by mutual interdependence. (Appendix 35)

The Methodists remind us of the necessity for repentance:

> All creation is the Lord's, and we are responsible for the ways in which we use and abuse it....Therefore, we repent

of our devastation of the physical and non-human world. (Appendix 40)

Hear the dramatic words of The Ecumenical Patriarch Dimitrios of the Orthodox Church:

> This Ecumenical Throne of Orthodoxy, keeper and proclaimer of the centuries-long spirit of the patristic tradition, and faithful interpreter of the eucharist and liturgical experience of the Orthodox Church, watches with great anxiety the merciless trampling down and destruction of the natural environment which is caused by human beings, with extremely dangerous consequences for the very survival of the natural world created by God. (Appendix 29)

The Lutherans use the language of theology:

> Christian concern for the environment is shaped by the Word of God spoken in creation, the Love of God hanging on a cross, the breath of God daily renewing the face of the Earth....We know care for the Earth to be a profoundly spiritual matter. (Appendix 27)

There are many interdenominational and interfaith groups as well. Examples are the National Council of Church's Eco-Justice Program (www.nccecojustice.org) and The Regeneration Project (www.theregenerationproject. org), both of which provide valuable resources for education and action.

The editors who worked during the 1970s on the most recent edition of the *Episcopal Book of Common Prayer* acknowledged this necessary broadening of our ethical frame of reference when they compiled the catechism (or "teaching") in the back of the book called "An Outline of the Faith." It begins with the question, "What are we by nature?" The response is, "We are part of God's creation, made in the image of God." There follows, "Q: What does it mean to be created in the image of God? A: It means that we are free to make choices: to love, to create, to reason, and to live in harmony with creation and with God." But we are left to wonder: how exactly can we learn to live in harmony?

Recently, the Episcopal Church's Committee on Science, Technology and Faith has taken the next step, and published a document for study in congregations—well worth study, of course, by individuals as well—called "A Catechism of Creation" (www.episcopalchurch.org/science), intended to bring the dialogue between science and theology into local worshiping communities. The goal of the scientists, theologians, and clergy who compiled this catechism was to remind people of the "importance of the glory of creation and the ways in which it touches people's faith every day." It is a treasure trove for those of us who are trying to listen to scientific language that may be foreign to us, but who need to understand it in order or respond to it, or to answer intelligently those who believe that religion and science are in conflict.

We learn that we do not have to choose between the concepts of faith we find in the Bible and the facts we hear from scientists. As the physicist and priest John Polkinghorne reminds us, while some of our ancestors may have asserted that "Holy Scripture containeth all things necessary to salvation,"[30] that does not mean that the Bible contains all necessary truths about everything else! It is nature itself, rather than the pages of any book, that reveals knowledge about the universe. The Bible proclaims another kind of truth, often through metaphor, poetry, and story.

The need for education about the issues of environmental stewardship is daunting, and the information available is more daunting still. When I began to work on this book, the information I had gathered over the years spilled out of my file drawers like the multiplying brooms in the story of the Sorcerer's Apprentice. Finally, thanks to Moses's tablets of the law, catechisms both old and new, and the useful websites of the information age, you will soon be traveling with me on a journey through the "thou shalts" of good ecological housekeeping for this, our *oikos*, or earthly home.

Ponder and Pray

Why do we all love the passage from Isaiah that begins this chapter? It is because of our longing for *shalom*, that peace that results when there is no fear and no enmity. The prophet's vision of a day when even predator and prey would live in peace evokes our longing for such a world, not only among the other creatures but among the members of that unruly species known as *homo sapiens*. All the commandments and catechisms of religion beckon us in that direction.

Read the Isaiah passage again, and sit quietly for a few minutes with the sense of *shalom* that it conveys. Then pray the prayer of St. Francis of Assisi:

Lord, make us instruments of your peace.
Where there is hatred, let us sow love;
where there is injury, pardon;
where there is discord, union;
where there is doubt, faith;
where there is sadness, joy.
Grant that we may not so much seek to be consoled as to console;
to be understood as to understand;
to be loved as to love.
For it is in giving that we receive;
it is in pardoning that we are pardoned;
and it is in dying that we are born to eternal life.
Amen.

3. No Other Gods

Then God spoke all these words: I am the Lord your God,
who brought you out of the land of Egypt, out of the house
of slavery. You shall have no other gods before me.

—Exodus 20:1-3

It is a helpful exercise to look at the story of Moses receiving the Ten Commandments on Sinai in the context of
the developing monotheistic faith of the Hebrew people,
and then to discover the relevance of the commandments'
guidelines for our own day. The Hebrew were wandering in
a landscape dotted with images of the gods favored by the
local tribes, whose worship was believed to ensure both the
stability of the political and social order and protection from
natural disasters. The Israelites broke with the polytheism
and mythology of the surrounding world by worshiping one
unseen God, Yahweh, whose power was revealed in the cosmic event of the Exodus, their flight from slavery in Egypt.

Surely, we do not need to be reminded of this commandment. Have you met any polytheists lately?

The answer is a resounding "yes," for polytheism
abounds. The gods are not as obvious as the pagan statues
in the shrines of the Canaanites, but they are more powerful. Take, for example, that bright and shining deity, money.
If we looked closely at the small print on our nickels, dimes
and dollars, we would find ourselves reminded that wealth

is not a god in whom we can invest all our trust. Despite that, the power of the marketplace all too often controls our society. The Rev. Daniel Orr, in a memorable sermon, told of a Nicaraguan minister who lamented that, in order to be in good standing with the rest of the world and thereby to get assistance, his country had to "play by the market's rules." These rules made them charge fees for public education and health services, to make loans only at high interest rates, to weaken the labor movement, and to create generous conditions for foreign access to natural resources. The market gave no thought to the well-being of an already impoverished country. The minister concluded, "Like the Canaanite God, Baal, in biblical Israel, this god has his attraction. When the sacrificial measures are adopted, they do generate wealth.... It is equally clear, however, that the market is a false god."[31]

Money, of course, is not in itself evil. I, for one, am grateful that we have enough of it to provide us with food, shelter, and clothing. It becomes a false god when people allow it to have ultimate control over their decisions, as the Nicaraguans have learned. They have had to obey its bidding, to the detriment of the well-being of the country and its people.

The money god exerts its power when economics trumps justice in political decisions about health care, education, or the environment. We enact its liturgies when anti-pollution controls are weakened because of cost, or when manufacturers balk at making more energy-efficient automobiles or appliances because their profits might suffer.

But what a short-sighted god the market is! Listen to some of its litanies: "Signing the Kyoto Agreement would wreck our economy"; "It is too costly to rebuild the Mississippi levees properly"; "Alternative sources of energy are too expensive." This short-sightedness does not take into account something called "full-cost accounting." Full-cost accounting involves considering both the entire present toll as well as the future toll of present decisions. Consider this shocking thought: despite our resistance to higher gasoline prices, the fact is that we are not paying nearly enough. The true cost of our profligate gasoline consumption in terms of global warming, air pollution, urban sprawl, automobile accidents, and the loss of human life in wars in oil-producing countries far away, is many times the price of whatever we happen to be paying at the pump. Full-cost accounting teaches us that this false god is not even practical.

The market god is one of many who lure humanity into idolatry. There are other false deities without number. An example is power, which is useful when wielded on behalf of other more enduring values, but dangerous when it becomes itself a god–hence, the saying, "Power corrupts." These false gods lure us into captivity, like the spider who said to the fly, "Will you come into my parlor?" Caught in their web, we no longer can reach out to the world with a sense of lasting and joyful hope in the future, to say nothing of present happiness.

Instead, their legacy is dissatisfaction, anxiety and fear.

And these can be contagious. I knew a second-grade teacher who one day noticed that a girl in her class seemed to be very depressed. When the teacher inquired gently about what was bothering her–Was it trouble at home? The death of a pet–her pupil (who must have listened more than her parents had expected to their dinner table conversation the evening before) gave a sigh. "I'm worried," she said, "about inflation."

I understand that for a while there was a bumper sticker that lightly mocked the worship of the marketplace: "Whoever dies with the most money, wins." Maybe a new one needs to be produced. It's a short but sweet saying from one of Christianity's most vibrant saints, Teresa of Avila, who led a life devoid of most of the qualities of comfort we would deem necessary today, but who was, nevertheless, if we can judge from her writings, utterly fulfilled and happy, and a woman far ahead of her time. It would read, "Whoever has God, lacks nothing."

Ponder and Pray

Take some time to relax, then read slowly St. Teresa's Prayer:

Let nothing disturb you,
Nothing dismay you;
All things pass,
but God never changes.
Whoever has God lacks nothing.

Reflect on the words, and also allow yourself time for just sitting silently in the presence of the God who continues to bring us out of enslavement to all the false gods of the world around us.

4. AMERICAN IDOLS

You shall not make for yourself an idol, whether in the form of anything that is in heaven above, or that is on the earth beneath, or that is in the water under the earth. You shall not bow down to them or worship them.

—*Exodus 20:4-5a*

Thus continues the Law from Sinai, directed to a wandering people journeying to a land where they would find statues of Baal and his female consort Baalat "on every green hill and under every green tree."

As one whose life and faith has been enriched by religious images in fresco, stained-glass, paint, mosaic, and stone, I find it difficult to relate to the second commandment. How can such a seemingly outmoded rule guide us today? Is there a truth behind it to which we need to pay attention?

I think there is. For us, who tend to see everything in the world through the lens of our narrow human concerns, it has to do with humility. While the "heathens" encountered by the Israelites may have carved and painted their idols to suit themselves, we often "paint" the whole world in the same manner–to suit ourselves. By so doing, we diminish our sense of God as well as our understanding of the mystery of God's creation.

In the days when my church musician husband moonlighted as the organist in a synagogue, I had the opportunity to tag along from time to time. There was something about the service that refreshed me in a way that few other worship experiences did, and I finally realized what it was. It was God-centered. *The Kaddish*, which was recited by the congregation in most of the services, summed it up:

> Let the glory of God be extolled, let His great name be hallowed in the world whose creation He willed. May His kingdom soon prevail....Let His great name be blessed for ever and ever. Let the name of the Holy One, blessed is He, be glorified, exalted and honored, though He is beyond all the praises, songs, and adorations that we can utter, and let us say: Amen.[32]

These words extolling God's mysterious grandeur made me feel the same calm I had experienced as a child in the Planetarium, my head tipped toward the stars. It was the *otherness* of God that quieted and reassured my spirit. Indeed, the Hebrew name of God, *Yahweh*, is not traditionally spoken in Judaism: it is too holy for speech. The God of the Jewish liturgy was not there primarily for our benefit. God was just *there*.

The church's teaching that God cares for us as a shepherd can often be distorted to mean that God is at our beck and call. This God is, in the words of the author J.B. Phillips, "too small." I loved the transcendence I encountered in Jewish worship, and never had any doubt that the God worshiped in the synagogue was the same one Jesus called "Abba." Although Jesus' relationship with "Abba" was intimate, his "Abba" was never cozy or undemanding, and certainly not a magical "god" who gives us anything we want if we pray hard enough.

I am reminded of a term from the discipline of environmental ethics: "intrinsic value." Things have intrinsic value when they are valuable in and of themselves, not merely because they are useful to us. As Aldo Leopold points out in his ground-breaking book, *A Sand County Almanac* (1949), just what deserves the label "intrinsic value" has changed. He uses as an example the return of Odysseus from the Trojan War, when the hero hanged the dozen slave-girls of his household suspected of misbehavior during his absence. The Greeks who first heard the tale of *The Odyssey* did not blink an eye: the girls were property, and the disposal of property, then as now, was a matter of expediency, not of right and wrong.[33] Yet today we are appalled at Odysseus' behavior, because—the era of slavery long past—we do not usually treat other people as if they had no worth, unless you count the faceless humans annihilated in our wars or devalued in other ways.

Leopold points out that ethics continued to evolve after the days of Odysseus, but he admits that even our own ethical system, which is based primarily on the relationship between individuals, still has a lot of growing to do. It was over fifty years ago that he wrote: "There is as yet no ethic dealing with man's relation to land and to the animals and plants which grow upon it." That idea sowed valuable seeds, for philosophers and theologians since then continue to wrestle to create a moral code that can guide our relationship with nature. He concludes: "It is inconceivable to me that an ethical relation to land can exist without love, respect and admiration for land, and a high regard for its value. By value, I of course mean something far broader than mere economic value: I mean value in the philosophical sense." He means, of course, "intrinsic value." And that leads us to ask some questions, as we explore this new generation of ethical thought. Does a forest have intrinsic value? Does it have a right to exist, just because it is, not merely because it provides lumber? Does a canyon have intrinsic value? Do monarch butterflies, or orioles, or buffalo, or salmon, or grizzly bears?

And, more brazenly, does *God?* Does God have value simply as God, not because God might grant our personal wishes when we pray for the sun to shine on our picnic at the same time the farmer next door is pleading for rain? Do we use God as a kind of club to hold over the heads of others who disagree with us, as we insist that "God is on our side"? Have we made God's very self a graven image, reflecting our own agendas?

I personally, would prefer to be on *God's* side. I would like God to just be, beyond any of my small agendas. And I would like to grant that right also to all the things the Creator has bestowed upon us, from rivers to ravens.

Ponder and Pray

The Book of Job in the Hebrew Bible, or "Old Testament," tackles the question we have been considering: do we "make God in our image," or is God beyond any possible images we could concoct, and even beyond the grasp of our finite minds?

The story begins with a description of Job as a righteous and prosperous man. Satan (not the "devil" at this point in Hebrew thought, but merely one of the heavenly beings who are gathered around the divine throne) comes to God "from going to and fro on the earth" and questions whether Job's goodness is sincere: does he serve God just because it is profitable to do so? God allows Satan to test Job, and Job suddenly finds "his fortune gone, his children dead, and himself residing on a dung heap at the edge of town where he fills his hours picking at his innumerable scabs and running sores."[34] To literally add insult to injury, three "friends" try to convince him that he must have sinned, otherwise he would not have been punished with ill fortune. Job continues to declare his innocence to his friends, and finally enters into conversation with God. Towards the end of this conversation there is a literary and spiritual masterpiece. I will vastly abridge it here, but suggest that you read it in its entirety. It is found in Job, beginning with Chapter 38 and continuing through Chapter 41.

> Then the Lord answered Job out of the whirlwind: 'Who is this that darkens counsel by words without knowledge? Gird up your loins like a man, I will question you, and you shall declare to me.
>
> Where were you when I laid the foundation of the earth? Who determined its measurements–surely you know! Or

who stretched the line upon it? On what were its bases sunk, or who laid its cornerstone when the morning stars sang together and all the heavenly beings shouted for joy?

He continues to address Job:

Have you entered into the springs of the sea, or walked in the recesses of the deep?....Have you entered the storehouses of the snow?....Can you bind the chains of the Pleiades, or loose the cords of Orion?....Can you lift up your voice to the clouds, so that a flood of waters may cover you?.... Can you hunt the prey for the lion, or satisfy the appetite of the young lions, when they crouch in their dens?....Do you know when the mountain goats give birth?...Do you give the horse its might?...Is it by your wisdom that the hawk soars, and spreads its wings toward the south?"

God does not "answer" Job's questions about why he is suffering, but God's speech puts Job's suffering into a new theological perspective.

Take some time with this wonderful text. What does it tell you about God? What does it tell you about your relationship to God?

5. Curses!

You shall not make wrongful use of the name of the Lord your God, for the Lord will not acquit anyone who misuses his name.

—*Exodus 20:7*

There are various translations of the commandment I first learned as "Thou shalt not take the Name of the Lord thy God in vain." Some prayer books use the more contemporary "You shall not invoke with malice the Name of the Lord your God," while a Jewish Torah commentary on my shelves renders it, "You shall not swear falsely by the name of the Lord your God." Confused? Wait until you read Everett Fox's 1983 translation (*The Five Books of Moses*): "You are not to take up the name of YHWH your God for emptiness."

This commandment is not just about the act of refraining from using God's name to punctuate our speech; it is what lies behind our tendency to swear. The translations "in vain," "with malice," "wrongful use," "swear falsely," and "for emptiness," all indicate that words themselves can have the power to diminish the human sense of God's holiness. The Israelites' understanding of ethics was built on this idea of holiness (leading one Rabbi Ibn Ezra to consider this third prohibition of vastly greater importance than any of those that follow[35]). The commandment reminds us, in the words of a Torah commentary, to safeguard "[God's] name from erosion and to maintain the sense of His holiness among his children."

This commandment brings to our conversation about environment ethics the reminder that behind our words lie our ideas and attitudes. That is, in fact, the reason that words have such power. Although we might once have chanted, "Sticks and stones can break my bones, but words will never hurt me," we probably have discovered a different version through experience: "Sticks and stones can break my bones, but words can hurt me forever." Broken bones can heal, while the wounds inflicted by taunts on the elementary school playground can fester for a lifetime. Psychologists tell us that children who hear only words of criticism from their parents grow up believing that they can't do anything right, for the idea has been absorbed as if by osmosis.

When we are adults, some of our assumptions about life are hidden under the surface of our consciousness, which is why the playground taunts and the hypercritical parents can be so damaging. This is also true of what is called our "paradigms," or imagined models of the way the world works. For example, before the sixteenth century, everyone assumed that the earth was the center of the universe. Then along came the astronomer Copernicus in 1512 and Galileo a half-century later, who insisted that our planet revolved around the sun. It is interesting to note that this so threatened the church's paradigm of the universe that it took years for theologians and prelates to catch up with reality.

There is an even more important shift in paradigm required of us today. We are being moved away from the outmoded notion that nature is here for our benefit and that its bounty is infinite. We are discovering that such a paradigm simply does not reflect reality. A new paradigm has been coming to birth: one which sounds tantalizingly familiar to those who know Genesis well. It contains the idea that our relationship to nature is one of stewardship, rather than "dominion." The latter word is a misunderstanding of God's intent that has caused an untold amount of damage over the centuries. The new paradigm is evocative of our natural childhood attitudes toward nature, and has long been assumed in the thought and practices of many indigenous peoples.

Now physicists who work in the field of quantum mechanics are discovering that, once two sub-atomic particles have interacted with each other, they remain related regardless of time and space, and the movement of one is echoed by the other. Physicists join the children and those peoples who have managed to remain mostly untouched by western thought, in telling us that–surprise!–*everything* is connected to *everything else*. We humans are part of the biotic community: our lives are interwoven, as if by a strong silken thread, into the entire web of life. While Copernicus and Galileo removed the earth from the center of the universe, this new vision of the world invites us to an even greater humility.

This paradigm honors the holiness of God through honoring the holiness of God's creation. We earth-creatures are not the center of the universe, and never were; and not only our words but our lives need to reflect that reality, or we put both human civilization and our planet itself at risk.

Individuals, institutions, corporations, and nations may resist this change, for all change is difficult. But I believe that one of the ways God is calling us to grow is through understanding the world around us in this new way. The birth pangs may be difficult. We may feel like the Pharisee Nicodemus, who came to Jesus by night, recoiling at Jesus' words: "No one can see the kingdom of God without being born from above."

Long before our time, the poet William Blake wrote,

This life's dim windows of the soul
Distort the heavens from pole to pole
And lead you to believe a lie
When you see with, not through the Eye.[36]

Seeking to understand the new paradigm will be like learning to see things through the eyes of the Creator, rather than through our own. We are invited into this new expression of the third commandment by the Spirit of God.

Ponder and Pray

Read Isaiah 43:18-19:

"Do not remember the former things, or consider the things of old.
I am about to do a new thing; now it springs forth, do you not perceive it?

*I will make a way in the wilderness **and** rivers in the desert."*

Take some time to let these words resonate within you. What is the *feeling* of this passage? Is there a sense of needing to let go? Of anticipation? Of surprise? Of going forward into uncharted territory? Does any of this describe the way you feel when certain ideas and attitudes begin to change?

God is stretching our minds and our hearts, as we move forward into the future. Pray these words from the Sarum Primer (1514):

God, be in my head, and in my understanding;
God, be in mine eyes, and in my looking;
God be in my mouth, and in my speaking;
God be in my heart, and in my thinking.
God be at my end, and at my departing."

6. R & R

*Remember the sabbath day, and keep it holy. Six days you
shall labor and do all your work. But the seventh day is a
sabbath to the Lord your God; you shall not do any work
– you, your son or your daughter, your male or female slave,
your livestock, or the alien resident in your towns. For in six
days the Lord made heaven and earth, the sea, and all that
is in them, but rested the seventh day; therefore the Lord
blessed the sabbath day and consecrated it.*

—*Exodus 20:8-11*

Observance of the Sabbath continues to be a center-
piece of Judaism. The setting sun on Friday night initiates
a period of twenty-four hours in which time itself becomes
transformed. I remember, as if it were yesterday, watching a
series about the world's great religions on public television
and hearing an Israeli Jew speak of the weekly Sabbath, the
"Queen of Days," set aside, not for *doing,* but for *delight.*
All week long, he would anticipate that period when he
could enjoy family, nature, and God. When I would accompany my husband to the synagogue on Friday night, I would
hear similar language:

> Those who keep the Sabbath and call it a delight shall
> rejoice in Your kingdom. All who hallow the seventh day
> shall be gladdened by Your goodness. This day is Israel's
> festival of the spirit, sanctified and blessed by You, the most

precious of days, a symbol of the joy of creation....Come with me to meet Shabbat, for ever a fountain of blessing. Still it flows, as from the start: the last of days, for which the first was made.[37]

Abraham Joshua Heschel, in his luminescent book *The Sabbath*, writes that the Sabbath itself is "a sanctuary which we build, a *sanctuary in time*." He evokes the second half of the commandment–"Six days shalt thou labor and do all thy work. But the seventh day is a sabbath to the Lord your God"–and reminds his readers that they, like the ancient Israelites, need to make room deliberately for the Sabbath, even, and *especially*, if they think they are too busy to do so. "Is it possible for a human being to do all his work in six days? Does not our work always remain incomplete? What the verse means to convey is: Rest on the Sabbath as if all your work were done."[38] Rest on the Sabbath *as if* all your work were done!

In his book, *Sabbath Time,* the priest and writer Tilden Edwards considers the Sabbath not merely as a particular day, but as a special quality of time. In my busy years at seminary, when I was juggling theological study, teaching, and domesticity, that book was a godsend. It freed me to take random moments for *shabbat*–the half hour on the commuter train, the ten-minute walk across town from the subway stop to seminary, or the interminable wait in line at the bank or supermarket. Before reading the book, I re-sented some of those moments, especially the last, as a waste of time, because I was not "doing something." Now, they were opportunities to just "be."

What does all this have to do with our relationship with the environment? The answer is a *great deal,* because the speed of life often conspires against our appreciation of Creation. We cannot acquire this appreciation merely by reading books or even by watching special programs on the Nature Channel, in which editors have increased the pace in order not to lose the viewers' attention. No, if we want to have a rapport with the natural world around us, we need to experience it ourselves. We need to slow down from time to time. When we do, we will see nature coming alive.

We can be creative about finding the Sabbath times within our daily activities of life. I have discovered that, in warm weather, one of mine is lunch time. When the weather becomes comfortable enough for me to sit outdoors, I put my lunch on a tray and sit on the glider facing the garden. At first, I *look out* at the garden. I study it like a painting. I see what has bloomed recently and spot what weeding or pruning will require some touch-up work on my part later that afternoon. But as I take time to settle down, I slowly begin to let go of my gardener's desire to control. I also switch from "photo" to "video" mode, and find myself *watching* the garden. I see the scene coming alive. The hummingbird zooms in on the nicotiana, the butterflies flutter around the buddleia, the sparrows take dust-baths, the squirrel peers down at me from the top branch of the crabapple, and the chipmunk scampers towards a long drink from the birdbath. I begin to feel the humidity of the air brushing my cheeks, carried by the same breeze that is causing the tall cleome to bend and bow like eighteenth-century aristocrats. I hear the rustle of the pampas grass at the edge of the garden; the scolding of the blue jay, who has spotted the neighbor's cat on the edge of the lawn; the intoxicating song of the male cardinal sitting like a red jewel in a dark green pine. I smell perfume from the lilacs at the edge of our property, the sweet fragrance of pansies and petunias in the patio planters, and just a hint of the horse farm on the outskirts of town. As I have quieted down, my senses have become more and more alive. Even the lunch is more tasty.

This may be one of the most important, and pleasurable, commandments of all when it comes to our ecological journey, for it is through this kind of Sabbath time that we discover and nurture our passion for preserving the natural world. Its activity can be summed up in three words: "Stop, Look, and Listen." And while some people travel far in order to claim this kind of sanctuary in time, we can claim it wherever we are. Even if we are confined to an apartment in the city, we can look out the window at the sky.

These contemplative moments change us within, so that we learn, little by little, that we do not need to control everything. As we let ourselves "just be," we can also let nature "just be."

Within the pages of the Bible, we find the concept of the jubilee year in Leviticus 25:10-12:

You shall hallow the fiftieth year and you shall proclaim

liberty throughout
the land to all its inhabitants. It shall be a jubilee for you: you
shall return,
every one of you, to your property and every one of you to
your family. That
fiftieth year shall be a jubilee for you: you shall not sow, or
reap the aftergrowth,
or harvest the unpruned vines. For it is a jubilee; it shall be
holy to you: you shall eat only what the field itself produces.

Whether the idea of a jubilee year–an extension of the idea of Sabbath rest–ever was put into practice by the Israelites is an unanswered question. But the compilers of Leviticus had the right idea. We need to rest from meddling with things from time to time, and just let them be. It will not be an unproductive time, however. Just the opposite. When we take time for sabbath or for jubilee, in the words of the former Presiding Bishop of the Episcopal Church, Frank Griswold, we will enter "a season of unfoldment in which God's blessing, compassion, and justice are unleashed, not from some remote heaven but from within the human heart."[39]

Ponder and Pray

Take a walk outdoors. Feel your connection to the earth as you take each step. Breathe deeply, as you inhale and exhale.

Now focus on each sense in turn. Stop for a moment and listen closely to all the sounds you hear, whether far away or close at hand. Walk some more and stop again. What do you smell? Continue walking, and, each time you pause, ask yourself another question. Is there a breeze? What is the temperature of the air? What textures can you feel, if it is warm enough for bare hands? Save "what can you see?" for last, since it is usually the first sense we use, and, as such, causes us to neglect the others.

If walking is impossible or difficult for you, you can do this exercise seated either outside, or inside, close to a window.

You will find, as you take walks in the future, that eventually it will no longer be necessary to structure the time in this way, for practice will have taught you to take in the natural world around you with all your senses. Remember always that this "sanctuary in time" awaits you, right outside your door.

7. THE FAMILY TREE

Honor your father and your mother, so that your days may be long in the land that the Lord your God is giving you.

—*Exodus 20:12*

The Israelites, a tribal people, knew that the well-being of their society was built on interdependence and trust. This was true, above all, of family. It would be many centuries before the emphasis on the individual, so taken for granted today, would begin to develop.

When I first learned this commandment in Sunday School, I interpreted it as "minding your mommy"; and its roots are, indeed, in the relationship between generations.

How can we interpret the importance of this generational relationship in the light of our theme of environmental responsibility? I believe that the Hebrew understanding of the individual as first and foremost part of a tribe and family can help temper our modern focus on our own personal well-being. It can help us realize that we are part of a geneology that has gone before us, and will continue after us, all being well. The difference is that today we need to turn our attention, not to those beloved parents and grandparents who preceded us, but to those generations who will follow us. Just as our sense of love must broaden into an ethics that includes more than other human beings, so our love must expand in *time*: into the future, to our grandchildren and great-grandchildren and on through the "greats" to the seventh generation (in the words of our Native American brothers and sisters) and, we would hope, beyond. As professors James Martin-Schramm and Robert Stivers write in their book, *Christian Environmental Ethics,* "The present generation takes in trust a legacy from the past with the responsibility of passing it on in better or at least no worse condition."[40]

This concept is the source of an extremely important word in the realm of environmental thought. It is the word "sustainable." Sustainability is, to put it simply, living in the present in such a way that the lives of our descendants are not jeopardized. A sustainable society is one that can meet its basic needs without compromising the basic needs of future generations.

Most of us who can do so hope to pass down a legacy to our children and grandchildren in the form of a financial estate that will lighten their future burdens. But there is an even more important legacy that we need to consider. It is the legacy of this planet's natural resources, including clean air, clear water, and fertile soil. Sadly, this is a legacy which we cannot, at this time, count on passing on to succeeding generations.

"The Catechism of Creation" (www.episcopalchurch. org/19021_58399_ENG_Print.html) suggests why Christians should be concerned about the state of God's earth:

> By the end of the twentieth century the human population
> had grown to six billion and by the mid twenty-first century

it may increase to nine billion. These huge increases and the economic development that accompany them are harming the earth's ability to support both the human population and the rest of God's creatures. Thousands of species are dying off as they are being hunted or their habitats degraded or destroyed. The earth's air, waters, forests and soils are suffering more and more pollution and depletion. Less land for farming is available to feed this huge and growing population, and disease, malnutrition and starvation are ever-present facts for millions of people. Greatly expanding usage of fossil fuels contributes to global warming, with consequences not yet fully understood but possibly severe for the whole earth. The very beauty of the earth is in peril. Furthermore, the vast majority of earth's human population is made up of the poor, those on whom God's heart is especially fixed, as Jesus taught, and they suffer in greater proportions from this 'groaning' of creation. (Rom. 8:22)

How did the world arrive at this sorry state? "The Catechism of Creation" asks the question,"Why is it difficult for human beings to love the creation as God loves it?"–and then responds:

We humans have fallen into sin...and expressions of greed, lust for power, neglect, and a willingness to turn a blind eye work against the mandate to be good stewards and keepers of God's good earth. Economic, political, and social structures and processes can also make this work difficult.

Often the damage is due to simple ignorance rather than deliberate sin. For example, we may not know the limits of growth until it is too late. Rich fishing banks can become depleted when fishermen's catches become so large that the fish cannot continue reproducing themselves at a sustainable rate. Sometimes it is due to new technologies and chemicals, an unwelcome gift of the industrial age. Our nation's legacy of fertile soil is diminishing by the day because of unsustainable farming methods by well-meaning farmers trying to make a living, who rely on chemicals for fertilizer and for weed and pest control rather than continually renewing the soil with organic matter and using biological methods to discourage problem plants and insects.

But all too often, the harm we have done as human beings is a symptom of what theologians have called "original sin," which I would describe as the innate egocentricity that seduces us into seeing the world only in terms of our own gratification.

There is one line in "The Catechism of Creation" that comforts me: "But contrition, repentance, confidence in God's forgiveness and the power of God's grace, and amendment of life provide a pathway for carrying out earth-keeping as a labor of love." The process begins within each of us, as we acknowledge our sorrow, our inevitable contributions to the depletion of our planet's resources, and our dependence upon God's forgiveness and the grace. That is the beginning of hope, for then comes action: what is called in the spiritual tradition "amendment of life." Those who are scientists, engineers, and technologists can use their gifts to contribute to the earth's care through scientific and technological innovations. Those with an artistic bent can write, or compose, or paint their contributions to the education and edification of this generation and those who follow. All of us can exercise stewardship by prudent and thrifty living that contributes to preserving other creatures and their habitats, restoring the earth's soils, air, and water, and protecting the places of beauty that heal our souls.

None of us can do this alone. Not only will others walk beside us, but there is a Source beyond us upon which we can depend. There are many forms of sustainable energy, among them solar collectors, windmills, and hydroelectric plants. But the greatest sustainable energy source is the one that will fuel our spirits. It will help us move forward courageously, even when things look daunting. It is ever with us, can never be depleted. It is the energy that swept through the upper room at Pentecost, that was breathed into the disciples by the Risen Christ, and that sent a handful of men out to all the known world with a message of hope and love: the abundant, never-ending energy of the Holy Spirit of God.

Ponder and Pray

What ways of prayer provide sustainable energy for your spirit?

Some people find solace in reciting the prayers both ancient and modern found in various prayer books and making them their own. Monastics and many clergy and laity recite the "daily offices": prayers said at regular intervals during the day.

Others are enriched and encouraged by opening the Bible. They read a passage of scripture slowly and meditatively, and ponder what it might mean for their own lives.

Others find that sitting quietly and letting go of any thoughts helps restore them. They focus on God's presence with them and within them, the prayer of just "being."

The varieties of prayer are endless. Listening to music, walking in the woods, service to others, all can build our relationship to our Creator and fill us with the energy and love that transforms ourselves and the world around us.

8. Murder!

You shall not murder.

—*Exodus 20:13*

"You shall not murder." How can this commandment help us better understand our relationship, not only with other human beings, but with the natural world beyond human society? It is an enormous topic. Over the centuries, there has been much heated discussion of the rights and wrongs of human behavior toward other sentient beings.

This discussion has been intriguingly broadened by recent research on animal behavior and perception. The very week I began working on this chapter, an article in the *New York Times* Sunday magazine featured a discussion on "animal personality" in an article entitled "The Animal Self." Of course, it doesn't take a research scientist to tell a pet owner that Fido and Fluffy have distinct character traits, but the subjects of this article were not dogs or cats. "Perched now, like entranced children, along the banks of their respective simulated streams, scientists are staring for hours at the least human of creatures." What are these creatures? They are Giant Pacific Octopusses, water striders, three-spined stickleback fish, and even fruit flies. Observing them, scientists have been struck by wide variations of individual behavior, such as shyness or aggression. Is the cause heredity or environment? Since these animals all have short life-spans, it has been possible to do research on this question, and scientists have come to the conclusion that it is both, just as is the case for human beings.

Such ground-breaking work, like the work done with whales, dolphins, and chimpanzees, will continue to raise controversy regarding the rights and wrongs of behavior toward species other than our own. At one extreme are energetic supporters of animal rights; at the other are those who believe that other animals were put on earth for human use; and in between there are innumerable gradations of opinion.

But there seems to be a growing general consensus about one thing: the issue of endangered species. It is wrong, most thinking people believe, to extinguish an entire species, as our country once did to the passenger pigeons, who were killed as pests and consumed for food.

What are the facts? Over the eons, there have been five waves of extinctions caused by natural disasters, as well as a lesser ongoing loss of certain species and replacement by others. The problem is that the natural rate of extinction has been vastly accelerated since humans arrived on the scene. Our weapons have included not only guns, nets, spears, and arrows, but habitat destruction and chemical poisoning. Since 1600, about five hundred animal species have been lost in the United States, while the natural rate of extinction would have resulted in about ten species. In Hawaii, half of the over two thousand native plants are threatened, and of sixty-eight species of birds unique to the island, forty-one have disappeared. We are told by the yearly global reports on the subject that we can expect up to a twenty percent loss of Earth's species within a few decades if present trends are not reversed.

Why should we care? There are several reasons. The one most often given is usefulness. Biodiversity (the presence of many different species) offers us vast material wealth, everything from pharmaceuticals to petroleum substitutes, and we have not even begun to discover them all.

Another is fear for the consequences on human society. Anne and Paul Ehrlich compare species extinction to popping rivets out of the wing of an airplane in which we are planning to travel. They conclude: "Only someone who did not know what rivets are for would knowingly patronize an airline with [those] rivet-popping practices... and only such a person would want to ride on Spaceship Earth when the rivets in its ecosystems were always being removed."[41]

The philosopher Holmes Rolston proposes a deeper reason:

> The main thing wrong is that extinction shuts down the generative processes. The wrong that humans are doing, or allowing to happen through carelessness, is stopping the historical gene flow in which the vitality of life is laid..... Every extinction is an incremental decay in this stopping of the flow of life, no small thing. Every extinction is a kind of superkilling.[42]

This superkilling is a moral offense against the God who is pictured in the Genesis stories as creating biodiversity in the first place: "creating creatures of *every kind*: cattle and creeping things and wild animals of the earth of *every kind*... and everything that creeps upon the ground of *every kind*" (Gen.1: 24). This is the playful God who, in the words of Psalm 104, made Leviathan, the great sea creature, so that it could "sport" in the ocean–although I prefer the earlier, less accurate translation of the Hebrew in the King James Version: "for the sport of it." Just for fun, in other words.

In the legend of Noah, who ensured the historical gene flow by taking two of each species aboard the Ark, God obviously expected Noah's descendants to refrain from exterminating the entire offspring of any of their shipmates. "Then God said to Noah..., 'As for me, I am establishing my covenant with you and your descendants after you, and with every living creature that is with you, the birds, the domestic animals, and every animal of the earth with you, as many as come out of the ark.'" (Gen. 9:8-11)

I hear echoes of the Book of Job: "But ask the animals, and they will teach you; the birds of the air, and they will tell you; ask the plants of the earth, and they will teach you; and the fish of the sea will declare to you. Who among all these does not know that the hand of the Lord has done this? In his hand is the life of every living thing and the breath of every human being." (Job.12: 7-10)

Learning to preserve the biodiversity of creation may take some education, and even some sacrifice, but it is, like most of the commandments, in our best interests: "Each species made extinct is forever slain, and each extinction incrementally erodes the regenerative powers on our planet."[43] More than that, we are tearing out some of the pages of the book of nature, which as we have seen, has long been believed to be one of the means that God is revealed to us. In the words of priest and theologian Thomas Berry, "We should be clear about what happens when we destroy the living forms of this planet. The first consequence is that we destroy modes of divine presence."[44]

Ponder and Pray

Include endangered species in your intercessions. You can obtain a list by going to www.worldwildlife.org. Here is the list I found when I visited the site recently:

Atlantic Salmon
Corals
Elephants
Great Apes
Marine Turtles
Monarchs
Pandas
Penguins
Pikas
Polar Bears
Rhinos
Snow Leopards
Tigers
Whales and Dolphins

I could picture them all, except for pikas. What were they? The World Wildlife Fund's site (www.worldwildlife. org/pikas) helped me out:

> The American pika, a small flower-gathering relative of the rabbit, may be one of the first mammals in North America known to fall victim to global warming if heat-trapping emissions are not reduced soon.... Many hikers, while passing through pika habitat...have heard these shy creatures call and whistle to each other. Since food is difficult to obtain in winter in the alpine environment, pikas cut, sundry, and later store vegetation for winter use in characteristic 'hay piles.' They are often called 'ecosystem engineers' because of their extensive haying activities....American pikas may be the 'canary in the coal mine' when it comes to the response of alpine and mountain systems to global warming.

I had become accustomed to my sorrow when I contemplated the extinction of the others, but, when I read about small shy flower-gathering rabbit relatives, of whose existence I had been completely ignorant, calling and whistling to one another in rocky alpine meadows, the thought that they could someday disappear altogether broke my heart.

9. ADULTERATION

You shall not commit adultery.

—Exodus 20:14

"You shall not commit adultery." Although some believe that this commandment was intended above all to protect a husband's property rights over his wife, and to ensure the legitimacy of his offspring, some students emphasize a different goal. "Purity of family life is [a] pillar of society as envisaged by the Bible. In time it became a distinguishing aspect of Israel's social structure, complementing the honor rendered to parents and the sense of responsibility felt for all members of the family."[45]

Just as honoring one's father and mother encouraged the stability of the relationship between parent and child, so the commandment forbidding adultery underscored the bond between husband and wife. Despite the very different sociological context from our own–men in biblical times were permitted to marry more than one wife, and concubinage (the acquisition of lesser-status wives) was also practiced–then, as now, it was believed that adultery sullied the purity of family life.

Adultery's close cousin, "adulterate," helps us shift our gaze beyond the ancient Hebrew family to the wider concerns of today. Adulterate means to "debase, spoil, taint, corrupt, or pollute," and that is what human beings have been busy doing to the world around them for centuries–but especially recently, whether through ignorance, greed, or carelessness. In so doing, we are sullying our *oikos*, our family home, in the same way that, on a smaller scale, we would do if we were to break the seventh commandment. My dictionary provides some examples of adulterating, such as debasing silver by adding copper, or diluting wine by sneaking in some water. In similar ways, we are adding ingredients to our natural resources–air, soil, and water–that do not belong.

The consequences are dangerous. Holmes Rolston put it this way back in 1988:

> Natural systems have considerable resilience and recuperative capacity; still, they may be pushed into deterioration and collapse. What will supersonic jets or aerosol cans do to the ozone layer? Where does all the DDT go, or the strontium 90? Humans sling natural chemicals around in unnatural volumes, allowing lead from gasoline, arsenic from pesticides, mercury from batteries, nitrogen from fertilizers, acids from coal-fired generators to find a way into places where they poison the life processes.[46]

Fortunately, because of the Clean Air Act of 1990, some progress has been made, but even that legislation has been in constant danger of being watered down, like the diluted wine in the stemmed glassware. One of the things we can do, therefore, is to communicate with our legislators about the need to maintain the Act at full strength.

When I was a college student, I had a friend whose family lived on the shore of Lake Erie. One summer day, I visited her home, eager to go for my first dip in one of the Great Lakes. Once I got there, I lost my enthusiasm quickly. The beach was littered with dead fish, the fallout of the industrial wastes being pumped into the lake just a few miles to the east. It was not until the Cuyahoga River burst into flame one day that action was finally taken to clean up the waters around Cleveland. Now I can drive twelve miles north on a hot July day to a clean beach and plunge into Lake Erie's restored waters.

The Hudson River boasts a similar success story, thanks to a banjo-playing troubadour of justice, Pete Seeger. The Hudson had become so polluted that the shad so prized by gourmets could not make it past the George Washington Bridge. Seeger, who lives about sixty miles upriver, decided to do something about it. He acquired a boat and named it the Clearwater. Its mission was to be raising consciousness about the deterioration of the Hudson. When our children were young, we once went for a sail on the Clearwater, boarding it, not upriver, but in lower Manhattan. It was a bright day, and the water sparkled in the sunlight. When we dropped anchor in order to "seine"–that is, send down a net to see what we could catch–the evidence underwater was not nearly as attractive. The catch consisted of no aquatic life at all–only old beer cans, soda bottles, and other garbage–the refuse of "civilization."

Twenty years later, I was to go seining again with the Clearwater crew, this time on the west bank of the river across from Poughkeepsie, New York. The occasion was a week-long course taught by the Clearwater organization, in the days when I was the coordinator of an Elderhostel program at Holy Cross Monastery (also located on the Hudson). This time, we caught small shells, a few fish, and very little debris. But if we had gone out farther and dredged deeper, we would have found something much more ominous than beer cans or soda bottles: PCBs from the General Electric plant far up the river.

PCBs, or polychlorinated biphenyls, are a mixture of individual chemicals, initially used as coolants and lubricants in transformers, capacitors, and other electrical equipment. They have not been produced in the United States since 1977, but they continue to adulterate our air, water, and soil. PCBs are sneaky: they are oily liquids or solids that are colorless to light yellow, can also exist as a vapor in air, and have no known telltale smell or taste. They also move around: they can travel long distances in the air, and can contaminate food–fish, meat, and dairy products–which we then eat. They are considered to be carcinogens, but also are the cause of birth defects and liver damage, among other ills.

The banning of PCBs was a significant step toward human health and that of our environment, but they are still lying at the bottom of the Hudson River close to the river bank where the path leading from the monastery ends.

But here there is another potential success story, a small sign of hope. In 2002, the Environmental Protection Agency decided to require GE to dredge the river. The corporation will construct a sediment transfer/processing facility, implement a habitat replacement and reconstruction program, and reimburse the EPA for the past and future costs of their pollution.

It is easy to be judgmental about GE's sins, but none of us should cast the first stone. Most of us, just by getting into our car and turning the ignition key, contribute to the brown smog that we can see from the window of an airplane (which is, in the meantime, contributing its share of the pollution) as we near any airport along the Northeast corridor. Through ignorance, we may also "commit adulteration" in all sorts of other ways, from dumping toxic cleaners into our toilets to poisoning our soil in order to get rid of dandelions.

Our faith journey in this time needs to include our learning about the impact of such practices. But first, we need to educate our hearts. George Maloney writes, "What we see around us in the pollution of the air, the streams, rivers, lakes, and oceans, our woods and forests and countryside, and in the jungles of our cities, is but an icon, a dramatic image, externalized, of what man is doing within himself in the unlimited expanses of his 'inner space.'"[47] These human hearts of ours surely yearn for clear air, clean water, and fertile soil. Becoming single-minded about our respect for God's creation—and refraining from adulterating it—might even be called a form of purity of heart.

Ponder and Pray

Take a census of your cleaning supplies. Read the labels on the containers, especially that fine print that follows the word "Warning!" Are there alternatives that you can use that would avoid putting further toxins in the air of your home, or in the water that goes down the sewer line?

You can find out by accessing www.care2.com/make-your-own-non-toxic-cleaning-kit.html. Try one of the suggestions, considering it a sacramental action.

10. Stop, Thief!

You shall not steal.

—*Exodus 20:15*

We all know that stealing means we are not to take things that do not belong to us–no shoplifting, pick-pocketing, or armed robbery. However, there are other, more subtle ways to steal. Ever since the prophet Jeremiah brought the word of the Lord to those who had grown "great and rich....fat and sleek" (Jer. 5:27-28), at the expense of others, there has been a broader interpretation of the eighth commandment. It is summed up in one word: justice.

It is unlikely that most of us have stolen recently in the first, narrow sense of the word: actually filching somebody else's belongings. But the sad truth is that probably every reader who lives in a First World country, myself included, is actually a thief.

I discovered my culpability during a lecture about one of the tools that environmentalists use to weigh justice. It is called an "ecological footprint." According to Mathis Wackernagel and William Rees, an ecological footprint is "an accounting tool that enables us to estimate the resource consumption and waste assimilation requirements of a defined human population or economy in terms of a corresponding productive land area."[48] In short, how many acres–fishing grounds, forests, pastures, or agricultural fields–does it take to maintain a given lifestyle?

The questionnaire that accompanies Wackernagel and Rees's book asks the reader to calculate their household's ecological footprint by recording a month's worth of consumption of food, consumer goods (such as clothes, paper products, and medicine), use of transportation, housing costs, and waste removal. When instructions for this project were distributed in my environmental studies class, the enterprise seemed daunting, and I postponed it.

I continued to be curious about my own impact, however, so I was relieved when I discovered that there was an abbreviated form on a website: www.MyFootprint.org. It takes only a few minutes to complete, and serves as a very approximate gauge of one person's consumption of earth's resources, unlike the more exhaustive quiz that can be found in conjunction with the Wackernagel-Rees book.

How virtuous I felt as I began the process of typing in my answers! We live in a modest home heated and cooled by sustainable energy, eat very little meat, and try to buy organic and local food and to use environmentally friendly new technologies whenever we are able. I didn't feel so virtuous when I finished it. After all was said and done, I discovered that my husband and I each need twenty-one acres to sustain our lifestyle, in part because of my frequent plane travel. (Since then, I have discovered that I can buy "carbon offsets" to neutralize this travel, through investing in a wind farm or forestry project.) According to the World Wildlife Fund's Living Planet Report 2006, which reports 2003 ecological footprints, we do a little bit better than the average U.S. citizen, who uses twenty-four acres per person. But we lag behind the Canadians just to the north, who are able to get by with nineteen acres, or the Italians with only ten. The Pakistanis, on the other hand, use only one-and-a-half acres per person.

The website added insult to injury by informing me that, if everyone lived the way I do, we would need 4.7 planets. Even people like us, who try to live what some consider to be a relatively simple life, are consuming much more than our fair share. It is as if each of us were invited to a party and cut ourselves a piece of chocolate cake that is over five times the size of what our hostess intended as she calculated how much she must bake for dessert.

The burden of guilt this information imposes upon our spirits is not necessarily helpful.

Our son Christopher wrote me this warning after I had e-mailed him this meditation:

"I suspect that anyone in the developed world is already doomed to scoring 'too high.' This is so inevitable as to have the potential of inspiring a helpless kind of shame, rather than hope for making a positive difference. Maybe it's a modern version of 'original sin,' except that the sin is a result of being born into the modern world, in which we are guilty before we can even speak." He continues that we need to put the focus on factors over which we, as individuals, may have very little or no control, but can only change through collective action. "Obviously, there's a place for both kinds of action—but the collective action (and even the individual action) is sometimes undertaken with more gusto if one isn't carrying around a load of shame for things that may not have appeared to be real choices in the first place."

It is not sufficient to pray, "Thy kingdom come": we need to help it happen, through our compassion, our lifestyles, and also our political action. My environmental ethics professor (whose name, remember, was Professor Care) believed that the only way we could live with a clear conscience was for each of us to give away a full ten percent of our wealth to those across the world who have so much less. We can also inform our elected leaders that we would feel more pride in our country if its priorities were adjusted in a similar fashion.

In addition, we can look at our daily lives—with the "gusto" to which Christopher calls us—and figure out how to decrease our footprint, however slight the difference might be. The Sierra Club's website (www.sierraclub.org/footprint) has some ideas. For example, drying twelve loads of laundry per month on the clothesline rather than in the dryer, showering three minutes less per day, or increasing by fifty percent the amount of organically grown food we eat, each saves a tenth of an acre. Driving only twenty miles less per week saves three-tenths of an acre, and eating a vegetarian dinner instead of meat once a week adds an entire half acre. The sum of these actions decreases one's footprint by more than a full acre, which doesn't sound like much to us, perhaps, but it would certainly make a difference to the Pakistani.

And it could make a tremendous difference cumulatively. On the Sierra Club web site, you are given an opportunity to pledge which footprint-diminishing actions you have decided to take. When the pledges were evaluated a couple of years ago, it was found that the choice of vegetarian dinners added up to145,000 fewer acres per year; and driving less each week saved 79,200. The entire amount pledged came to 520,100 acres–no small amount. As we summon the gusto to tread more lightly, both individually and collectively, on this earth, and as developing technologies help us lessen our consumption of earth's resources, perhaps the time will come when we privileged citizens of the so-called First World will no longer need to blush with shame when we hear the eighth commandment.

Ponder and Pray

Access www.sierraclub.org/footprint. Fill out the simple questionnaire in order to discover your ecological footprint. Then look at the ideas provided to help decrease your impact on the earth. Take time to think about which ideas are reasonable for you to act upon. If you decide to take one or more of the suggested steps, offer the action to God as a way of expressing compassion for your brothers and sisters around the world, in gratitude for the abundance of creation that all are meant to share.

11. The Emperor's New Clothes

You shall not bear false witness against your neighbor.

—*Exodus 20:16*

If not bearing false witness meant only "don't tell lies," obeying–or knowing when we are disobeying–this commandment might be easy. But what if we think of this commandment as a "thou shalt," instead? "Thou shalt tell the truth": even if it is a hard truth, painful for others to hear, you shall not keep silent. And what if it means even more? What if it means we must also face the truth, rather than avoiding it?

Throughout the years, I have heard certain information about the degradation of the environment of which I would have preferred to be ignorant. My reluctance to acknowledge this information did not make it go away. When I was a teenager, I did not want to know that several municipal sewage systems flowed into Long Island Sound, because, when we went for a family sail and became becalmed, I liked to jump off the boat to swim in the salty water. When we were planning to move to Oberlin, I resisted the information that air quality was poor in the region immediately to our north. Even now, when I stand in front of the fish section of our local supermarket, I wish that there were not a list of species under the headings of "best choices" "proceed with caution" and "avoid" on our kitchen bulletin board.

We all remember the days, not long ago, when the topic of global warming was controversial. Climatologists–who were simply recording changing weather phenomena and then applying scientific research methods to ascertain the possible causes–were often confronted by intense and often highly emotional resistance on the part of those who didn't want to believe what they heard. Now, any resisters who remain can no longer wax quite so eloquent, for the increased fury the weather has unleashed on many parts of the earth is finally convincing even the most hardened disbelievers. Unfortunately, resistance had already taken its toll through delays in strengthening emissions guidelines or developing new technologies.

I am reminded of Hans Christian Anderson's story, "The Emperor's New Clothes." I will retell it below, in my own words.

Once upon a time, there was an emperor who was exceedingly fond of new clothes. One day, two swindlers came to town who said they were weavers who made magnificent fabrics of fine colors and patterns. Their fabrics were distinguished by the phenomenon that the cloth, once woven, was invisible to anyone who was either unfit for his office or unusually stupid.

Naturally, the Emperor wanted such amazing clothes, so he paid the two swindlers a large sum of money and they started to work. They set up two looms and demanded the finest silk, which went into their traveling bags, while they worked with empty looms day and night.

The Emperor sent various ministers and officials to ob-serve the weavers, and the swindlers would point to the empty looms and invite their visitors to examine the intri-cate patterns. None of the ministers and officials dared to say, "There's nothing there!" for fear of being thought stu-pid or undeserving of his post. Finally the Emperor himself went to see the work in progress. He followed the example of the ministers and officials, for fear of appearing unwor-thy of his post: "Oh! It's very pretty!" Everyone agreed that it would be the perfect outfit for the Emperor to wear in the great procession he was to lead the following day.

The swindlers "worked" all night before the procession, burning "more than sixteen candles." In the morning, they pretended to take the cloth off the loom, made cuts in the air with huge scissors, and said, "Now the Emperor's new clothes are ready for him," explaining that they were so fine, "light as a spider web," that he would almost think he had nothing on.

The Emperor undressed, and the swindlers pretended to put his new clothes on him, one garment after another, finish-ing with a mantel and its long train, as the Emperor turned round and round before the mirror. On all sides, people said, "That pattern, so perfect! Those colors, so suitable!"

Soon it was time for the procession. The noblemen who were to carry his train stooped low and reached down for the imaginary train, and off went the Emperor under his splendid canopy. Everyone in the streets acclaimed their ruler and admired his new clothes. "Oh, how fine are the Emperor's new clothes! Don't they fit him to perfection?

And see his long train!"

"*But he hasn't got anything on,*" a little child said.

"Did you ever hear such innocent prattle?" said his father. But the people whispered to one another what the child had said, until the whole town cried out at last, "*But he hasn't got anything on!*"

The tale ends chillingly:

The Emperor shivered, for he suspected they were right. But he thought, "This procession has got to go on." So he walked more proudly than ever, as his noblemen held high the train that wasn't there at all.[49]

The "Emperors" of the world are those political leaders and CEOs who persist in refusing to see the naked truth. The admiring officials and ministers and townspeople are those who refuse to bear witness to the truth. We all have the capacity to hide our heads in the sand, for it is part of our nature to shrink from paying attention to problems that will disturb or inconvenience us. How stubbornly we human beings want to believe that everything is all right with the world! How much we want to keep on doing business as usual, rather than responding to environmental changes that will probably affect our own lives at some point, and certainly will affect our children's and grandchildren's lives.

It is the little child who saves us: the little child born in Bethlehem over two millennia ago, whose ministry bore witness to truth, and whose ongoing presence gives us courage to bear witness as well. And so, through God's grace, may we all be emboldened to speak out: "*But he hasn't got anything on!*"

Ponder and Pray

Have there ever been hard truths that you have resisted acknowledging? Or have you acknowledged them, yet felt timid about speaking out about them? Pray the following prayer, asking for courage to be included among those who "speak where many listen" and "write what many read."

"Almighty God, you proclaim your truth in every age by many voices. Direct in our time, we pray, those who speak where many listen and write what many read; that they may do their part in making the heart of this people wise, its mind sound, and its will righteous, to the honor of Jesus Christ our Lord. Amen." (*The Book of Common Prayer,* p. 827)

12. Consuming Passions

You shall not covet your neighbor's house; you shall not covet your neighbor's wife, or male or female slave, or ox, or donkey, or anything that belongs to your neighbor.

—Exodus 20:17

The word "covet" is not used lightly here, the way we might say to a friend, "I covet that dress," for the word "house" didn't mean merely your nomadic neighbor's tent, but everything he owned, from wives to slaves to livestock. Coveting meant that you hoped to dispossess your neighbor. But you hadn't necessarily done it yet; you had just thought about it. Of all the commandments, this is the most inward, directed to the heart.

Coveting does not make our hearts comfortable; it fills them with dissatisfaction. Of all the commandments, this one is perhaps the most subversive. That is because the "health" of the marketplace is based on coveting. We are told that buying things is patriotic because we need to support the economy, and many people are all too ready to support it by running up immense credit card debts.

Such a focus on economics harms both our society and ourselves. The propaganda of marketers is expensive; an obscene amount of money is spent on generating a demand for products, as compared to the amount spent on health care and education. Advertising can be a subtle form of brainwashing, making us want things that it may never have occurred to us to desire. As our ecological footprint grows larger through this accumulation of possessions, our hearts grow smaller, for we inevitably discover that the material things we thought would satisfy us fail to do so.

When our perspective is tainted by coveting what we do not yet own, we are like the penitents in the fifth ring of the Purgatorio, the middle section of Dante's poetic journey through the afterlife that can also be read as a wise guide to the life of the spirit. As Dante and his companion, the poet Virgil, climb the Mountain of Purgatorio, they encounter people "stretched out here weeping, their faces turned towards the ground." Their trials expiate their earth-bound sin, for, in the words of Dorothy Sayers, their souls were so fettered by covetousness on earth "that they now can see nothing but the earth on which they once set store."[50]

Alan Durning, author of the book, *How Much Is Enough?: The Consumer Society and the Future of the Earth*, would agree that setting store on things of earth is not a satisfying goal, although he puts it in more contemporary terms:

> Ironically, high consumption is a mixed blessing in human terms....People living in the nineties are on average four-and-a-half times richer than their great-grandparents were at the turn of the century, but they are not four-and-a-half times happier. Psychological evidence shows that the relationship between consumption and personal happiness is weak. Worse, two primary sources of human fulfill-

ment–social relations and leisure–appear to have withered or stagnated in the rush to riches. Thus many of us in the consumer society have a sense that our world of plenty is somehow hollow–that, hoodwinked by a consumerist culture, we have been fruitlessly attempting to satisfy with material things what are essentially social, psychological, and spiritual needs.[51]

Of course, someone had said that long before: "Do not store up for yourselves treasures on earth, where moth and rust consume and where thieves break in and steal; but store up for yourselves treasures in heaven, where neither moth nor rust consumes and where thieves do not break in and steal. For where your treasure is, there your heart will be also." (Matt. 6: 19-21)

Where your treasure is, there your heart will be also. Joe Dominguez and Vicki Robin, in their book *Your Money or Your Life,* write about "making a dying" rather than making a living. They suggest calculating the cost of an item we wish to buy in terms of the *hours of work* required to earn enough to afford the item. When we have tallied how many hours of "life-energy" an item costs, we are likely to think twice about acquiring things we do not need. They suggest steps towards reaching a sustainable balance between work and consumption: living within our means, taking care of what we have, not replacing something until it is worn out, buying used items, and researching the value, quality, and durability of what we purchase. I like to remind myself of these guidelines when an unnecessary item catches my eye.

Will it just add to the clutter that looms in every household—a fate, the authors tell us, that is "worse than dearth." Am I willing to spend my "life-energy" hours for it?

How much is enough? It is part of life's journey to learn what things are worth wishing for, and which are not. As a child, I truly coveted my friend Peggy's pink velvet jodhpurs, which she would wear when she took horse-back riding lessons at a nearby stable. I also coveted those riding lessons. My parents said "No": they were already paying for piano, dance, and art lessons. But how I wanted those jodhpurs. When I recently confessed this fixation to Peggy, she didn't even remember them. I suppose they had not given her lasting satisfaction, a truth I would have soon realized if my parents had granted my wish.

Covetousness not only contributes to the gulf between the rich and the poor, but is toxic to our hearts, stealing our contentment.

When I was commuting to General Seminary, I often would drive to the city with Mary Louise, an intelligent and wise friend. Our talks in the car were an integral part of my theological education. She summed up the Tenth Commandment one day, by quoting something her mother had said to her when Mary Louise was still a child: "Happiness is wanting what you have."

Happiness is wanting what you have! Amen!

Ponder and Pray

The great antidote to covetousness is gratitude. One can use a beloved traditional prayer from the seventeenth century, such as "The General Thanksgiving":

Almighty God, Father of all mercies,
we your unworthy servants give you humble thanks
for all your goodness and loving-kindness
to us and to all whom you have made.
We bless you for our creation, preservation,
and all the blessings of this life;
but above all for your immeasurable love
in the redemption of the world by our Lord Jesus Christ;
for the means of grace, and for the hope of glory.
And, we pray, give us such an awareness of your mercies,
that with truly thankful hearts we may show forth your
praise,
not only with our lips, but in our lives,
by giving up our selves to your service,
and by walking before you
in holiness and righteousness all our days;
through Jesus Christ our lord,
to whom, with you and the Holy Spirit,
be honor and glory throughout all ages. Amen

(The Book of Common Prayer, p. 101)

We can address God less formally, as my grandchildren do as they say grace before meals, telling God the things that give them happiness, from ice cream to favorite toys.

Most of all, we can cultivate the habit of gratitude, saying "thank you" in our hearts throughout the day, when a spouse returns safely from driving on icy roads, when the first green shoots of spring flowers catch our eye, or just when we take a moment to be conscious of the gift of being alive.

ACTION

*What good is it, my brothers and sisters, if you say you have
faith but do not have works? Can faith save you? If a brother
or sister is naked and lacks daily food, and one of you says
to them, "Go in peace; keep warm and eat your fill," and
yet you do not supply their bodily needs, what is the good of
that? So faith by itself, if it has no works, is dead.*

—James 1:14-17

How do we practice what we preach? How do we live
what we believe? This section provides a few examples,
among the many that are available in other sources. We begin with a chapter on ecological design, the common thread
that weaves together all our efforts. We will then consider
how the following can be examples of ecological design: a
building, a furnace, a car, a meal, a light bulb, the contents
of our garbage can, and our willingness to speak out about
what we believe. How can these even become sacramental:
outward expressions of our inner beliefs?

1. Ecological Design

This planet has been delivered wholly assembled and in perfect working condition, and is intended for fully automatic and trouble-free operation in orbit around its star, the Sun.

However, to ensure proper functioning, all passengers are requested to familiarize themselves fully with the following instructions. Loss or even temporary misplacement of these instructions may result in calamity. Passengers who must proceed without the benefit of these rules are likely to cause considerable damage before they can learn the proper operating procedures for themselves...

Upon close examination, this planet will be found to consist of complex and fascinating detail in design and structure. Some passengers, upon discovering these details in the past, have attempted to replicate or improve the design and structure, or have even claimed to have invented them. The Manufacturer, having among other things invented the opposable thumb, may be amused by this. It is reliably reported that at this point, however, it appears to the Manufacturer that a full panoply of consequences of this thumb idea will not be without an element of unwelcome surprise.[52]

—David Brower, "The Third Planet: Operating Instructions"

I am not by nature a scientist. When I had to write down what my "hobbies" were in elementary school, I remember writing "nature," but it wasn't because I really studied it. I just took pleasure in it. On my childhood walks through the woods, I drank in the beauty of trees, mosses, and wildflowers, rather than writing in a notebook the names of what I'd observed. My bent is artistic and philosophical: I love color, texture, music, and meaning.

For that reason, when I first heard our professor mention the phrase "ecological design," I finally felt right at home. "Ecological design," he told us, "requires the ability to comprehend patterns that connect, which means getting beyond the boxes we call disciplines, to see things in their larger context. Ecological design is the careful meshing of human purposes with the larger patterns and flows of the natural world, and the careful study of those patterns and flows to inform human purposes."[53]

Ecological design (unlike "intelligent design") is not a theory about how things came to be, but an observation of the way things are. It is about the relationships between things. I suppose I have always resonated to this idea: I distinctly remember my excitement at learning in an elementary school classroom that trees "breathe in" the carbon dioxide that we exhale, and then "breathe out" the oxygen upon which we so much depend for life.

Like love, ecological design provides us with a lens through which to perceive our proper relationship with the created order. Knowing how things actually work can guide us into right decisions, and ignoring the designs embedded in nature can lead to harm. Architect William McDonough writes:

> Could you design a system for me that produces billions of pounds of finely hazardous toxic material and put it in your soil, your air, and your water every year? Could you design a system...that measures your prosperity by how much natural capital [i.e. coal, oil, forests, soil] you can dig up, cut down, bury, burn, otherwise destroy?...While you're at it, produce a few items so highly toxic they will require thousands of generations to maintain constant vigilance while living in terror....Is this ethical?[54]

Obviously it is not. The antidote? I hear David Orr's voice again: "The crisis is foremost one of thought, perception, imagination, intellectual priorities, and loyalties.... Poor design results from poorly equipped minds. Good design can only be done by people who understand harmony, patterns, and systems."[55]

I should have studied more science. When scientists talk like this I can relate to them. I can appreciate what Mc-Donough calls the necessary "new design assignment" for humanity: "Design a system that doesn't produce any hazardous toxic material....Measure prosperity by how much natural capital you can put into constant closed cycles that are healthy and propitious, and measure progress by how few buildings you have that have smokestacks....What we're talking about here is not necessarily just becoming more efficient. We are not just celebrating efficiency. What we're going to do is celebrate abundance."[56]

I like to think of ecological design as a kind of choreography. Because we have what theologians call "free will," we can choose whether or not to dance according to its patterns. Imagine that you have joined such a dance on a great stage, and you decide to make up your own choreography, without any regard to what is going on around you. You probably will collide with other dancers, creating danger both for them and yourself. You may wish you could change their dance patterns to suit your own tastes, but you do not have the power to do so.

Examples of colliding with the choreography of the natural order are too many to enumerate. We could start with Jesus's story of the house built on sand, "and the rain fell, and the floods came, and the winds blew and beat against that house, and it fell–and great was its fall!" (Matt. 7:26-27) People still literally build their houses on sand, forgetting that it is in the nature of sand to shift when buffeted by wind and waves. My aunt and uncle used to spend summers in a cottage on Fire Island, off the coast of Long Island. The view towards the ocean was slightly obscured by cottages built closer to the beach. The last time I heard, their former cottage is right at the edge of the dunes–unless it, too, has been washed away by now.

I think that every experienced gardener has experienced what it means to respect nature's design. Mostly, we learn it when things simply do *not* work. When we first moved here, I wanted to plant a rhubarb bed toward the back of our property. I double-dug the soil, amended it with compost and manure, planted the seedlings, and waited eagerly for the harvest. Nothing came up. One day after a heavy rain, we strolled near the failed rhubarb bed and discovered that the earth beneath our feet was so soggy that it felt like walking on a soft mattress. Since this town was built on a wetland, it was apparent that our rhubarb had simply drowned! What does grow in those damp parts of our yard are the beautiful purple Siberian iris that thrive so well at the edges of ponds, so now we feast on the vision of their blossoms instead of feasting on rhubarb.

Nature eventually wins, when we try to impose our own designs on her. The city of New Orleans endured safely for a time, until the inevitable floods and winds came. What if humans had refrained from building their city on the flood plains over which it is in the nature of rivers to flow when the water level becomes too high? Would the outcome have been different if the Mississippi had been allowed to form the delta that it is in the nature of rivers to create?

The fertility of our farmlands may endure for a while, unless the topsoil is finally completely washed away because of poor agricultural practices that do not reflect the pattern of nature. What if the farmland had been continuously amended with organic matter all along, as happens naturally in a meadow or forest, where the soil is continuously built up rather than depleted?

Development in the American Southwest will continue until it becomes apparent that the water supply, so ingeniously designed to come from elsewhere, will run out. What if we had recognized our limits, and refrained from building sprawling cities in the desert, despite the lure of desert beauty and bright weather?

The good news is that we human beings have the capacity to learn. Even if we are not ourselves scientists, we can respond to scientific evidence by thinking and acting in new ways, using our intelligence and imagination. William McDonough writes, "We should take this creative thing that we have in us–it's a sacred thing, it's a gift–and we should celebrate our abundance."[57]

Ponder and Pray

Consider any recent so-called "natural" disaster. Is there a way in which ignoring ecological design contributed to it? Pray for those who were affected, and pray also that the people who help to heal and rebuild will do so in accord with nature's intended design. Hold this all before God, and pray this prayer from the Lakota Indian tradition:

Grandfather, Great Spirit,
you have always been, and before you nothing has been.
There is no one to pray to but you.
The star nations all over the heaven are yours,
and yours are the grasses of the earth.
You are older than all need, older than all pain and prayer.
Grandfather, Great Spirit,
fill us with light.
Give us strength to understand and eyes to see.
Teach us to walk the soft earth as relatives to all that live.
Help us, for without you we are nothing.[58]

2. A Building Like a Tree

How dear to me is your dwelling, O Lord of hosts!
My soul has a desire and longing for the courts of the Lord;
my heart and my flesh rejoice in the living God.

The sparrow has found her a house
and the swallow a nest where she may lay her young;
by the side of your altars, O Lord of hosts,
my King and my God.

Happy are they who dwell in your house!
They will always be praising you.

—*Psalm 84, 1-3*

From my comfortable perch in the twenty-first century, I admire the Middle Ages. The beauty and power of medieval art, architecture, music, and faith cause me to overlook the downside–medically, politically, and socially–of actually living in that era. My ardor was ignited by some of the great Gothic cathedrals of Europe, discovered in my year as a student studying and traveling in France and Great Britain. When I enter those history-laden prayer-permeated sacred spaces, so vibrant with a spirituality expressed through stone, structure, and stained glass, I feel enveloped by the holy.

These buildings were erected to serve not merely as worship spaces, but as community gathering places and teaching tools. The medieval cathedral was the outward, visible equivalent of Thomas Aquinas's *Summa Theologica*, the "high medieval synthesis" expressing the order, hierarchical structure, and beauty of the worldview of its time. Worshipers who entered might have glanced upwards as they walked beneath a portal depicting the Last Judgment, replete with saints and sinners. They would see other statues flanking the doors: biblical characters like Abraham and Isaac, Mary Magdalene, King David playing his harp, and Mary the Mother of Jesus. Once inside, the congregation was surrounded by other depictions of the sacred story in roof bosses, corbels, and sculptures. The red, blue, and gold light that dappled the cathedral's stone pavement passed through illustrations of more biblical stories. Even those worshipers who were illiterate knew something about scripture, because they "entered" it each Sunday. As they gathered in the vast nave, looking up towards the altar where the distant clergy presided, they absorbed through their pores the medieval point of view.

Are there buildings that express today's worldview in similar fashion? In my more cynical moments, I would choose as contenders the cathedrals of consumerism–big box stores, or the financial maelstrom called the New York Stock Exchange. But these express only the less admirable addictions of our society: the accumulation of possessions and the pursuit of wealth.

Fortunately for the future of the planet, today there exist buildings that express other values: good stewardship that includes the natural world, and the belief that human beings thrive best when they can draw upon nature's wisdom. Several years ago, such a building–the Adam Joseph Lewis Center for Environmental Studies–was constructed right down the road from us on the Oberlin College campus.

This building, like the medieval cathedral, grew out of community. It saw first light in an environmental architecture class. A student proposed a project that would help people re-think the whole concept of buildings. Gradually, the idea took shape. Idea was added to idea, as students, faculty, and townspeople gathered in regular meetings or "charrettes" to brainstorm about the project. The environmental center was to serve the entire community, not just the college, and was to be built of sustainable materials and utilize sustainable energy.

Funding was procured and William McDonough, a noted spokesperson for green building design, was chosen as architect. In the program distributed at the groundbreaking, he wrote: "The design for the building is both 'restorative' and 'regenerative'; it addresses how architectural design may reverse the environmental stresses brought on by the industrial revolution. To this end, we have considered how the building can be fecund, like a tree, accruing solar income to the benefit of living systems and absorbing water quickly and releasing it in a healthy state."

The community watched with interest as the open space between two dormitories turned into a building project, and an elegantly simple building that could well have been claimed by the Shakers began to rise. Those who contributed to it included some visionary philanthropists and a number of the most skilled minds in the technological field, from NASA staff to a cadre of landscape architects, civil and structural engineers, and specialists in lighting, acoustics, energy, and solar design. Just one week short of two years after the ground-breaking, the Lewis Center was dedicated.

Like a tree, the building relies on the sun. Solar energy is harnessed both through photovoltaic cells on the building's south-facing roof and an efficient "passive" solar design that provides warmth in the winter and shade in the summer. Lights are not activated until a sensor sends the message that someone needs them. A biological wastewater system, or "Living Machine," adjoins the airy atrium. It looks like a miniature jungle, and replaces chemical treatment of wastewater with a series of ponds in which diverse communities of living organisms remove harmful bacteria from the water by replicating a natural wetland. All of the materials in the building are sustainable, durable, and low-maintenance. The walls of the auditorium are made from wheatstraw and smell like a sunny summer day in the country. The auditorium's carpeting and upholstery are leased from the manufacturer, who will take them back and re-use them to make new fabric when they begin to look worn. Surrounding the building are an orchard, a wetland, a garden, a grove of indigenous trees, and a sun plaza, in the center of which stands a tall pole that maps the solar year as its shadow falls on the ground below.

When I enter the Lewis Center, I am entering a new kind of "cathedral" that speaks the language we need to hear now. Without any words, it teaches us through its very fabric and design about sustainability, the intricate web of life, conservation, and beauty. Like the medieval cathedral that inspired peasants and pilgrims through its unspoken language of faith, the Lewis Center speaks to its surrounding community about hope, and is, therefore, like its medieval ancestor, a holy space, one that both informs and inspires the people of today.

Ponder and Pray

Think about spaces that have had an impact on your spirit. They can be homes, or places of worship, or even places of business.

Picture each one, and ask yourself what messages they have conveyed. What has impressed you about them?

Perhaps as a child you built a clubhouse, as my brother and his friends did, to provide an oasis where "no girls were allowed." You may remember a house you once lived in, like the airy Victorian in which our children grew up. What impressed me about living there was not only its simple elegance but its connection with local history; it had been the first telephone exchange in our village, and there were round wooden circles in the floor where the cables had once been.

Perhaps you have visited the United Nations in New York City, where the building itself made your spirit expand with hope, for the architecture and art proclaim its mission of peace. Or you may have visited the architectural duet between nature and house that is Frank Lloyd Wright's "Fallingwater," nestled so perfectly above a waterfall, and it has taught you about integrating nature itself into the design of a home.

What places of worship have most affected you, and why? What kinds of messages did they give you, through their architecture and art?

If you could start from scratch and design your ideal structure, whether home, place of worship, or something else, what would it look like? How would you try to include your stewardship of God's creation? In what ways could the building convey the message of the Psalm, "How dear to me is your dwelling, O Lord of hosts!"

3. STRANGELY WARMED

Twist and get whole.
Bend and get straight.
Be empty and get filled.
Be worn and get renewed.
Have little; get much.

—*Lao Tzu* [59]

The great medieval cathedrals inspired the peasants and princes who came as pilgrims. They took home with them an increased desire to live in harmony with what the cathedral had taught them about the way of Christ. The Lewis Center, likewise, has been an influence in our community and beyond.

I, for one, had never realized the extent of the environmental impact for good or ill of the structures in which we live, study, and work. I had taken for granted that the villains in the scenario of environmental degradation were industry and transportation, not ordinary structures like the homes we live in. I learned instead that houses have the greatest impact of all, simply because there are so many of them.

We reacted to this information by taking advantage of a free energy audit offered by the city –a kind of CAT scan for the home that detects areas of energy loss. Two technicians arrived with a large exhaust fan that fit into the framework of our front door, creating a tight seal. To the accompaniment of its roar once they turned it on, they prowled around the inner walls and windows with a device that puffs out "smoke" in order to detect heat leakage, and then used an infrared camera to reveal other cold areas. Afterwards, they wrote us a prescription for increased energy-efficiency. We were told what we already suspected: that we needed to replace our ill-fitting guestroom windows on the south and the windy west side of our home, but that simple caulking of other leaks would suffice.

The year after the Lewis Center was built, our venerable furnace began to falter. We called Tom from a local heating and cooling company for help. As we sat with him at our dining room table with pamphlets spread before us, considering how to purchase the most efficient furnace possible–and whether we could afford the cost (and guilt) of including air-conditioning–Tom said very quietly, "Maybe you'd like to consider geothermal."

The happy quickening of my heartbeat told me what our decision would be, since the Lewis Center had already taught us about geothermal heat and cooling. There, twenty-four closed-loop geothermal wells are connected to heat pumps within the building, harnessing the internal temperature of the Earth for the purpose of both cooling and heating. We decided to follow suit, although we would need only four wells.

It was not long before two local farmers, whose fields were still too muddy to plow, parked their equipment in the street in front of our house. They were to dig our wells one-hundred-fifty feet deep, about twelve feet apart. For six days, the rigs in our front yard suggested to passers-by that we might have discovered a vein of oil, as the drills bored their way through the heavy clay which so often confounds local gardeners. At about seventy-five feet, they hit a vein of sand, then, awhile afterwards, rock–giving us a short survey of the geology of this once-mountainous, then oceanic, part of the world. It is hard to imagine that, millions of years ago, this flat agricultural patchwork had been the site of mountains higher than the Himalayas. After millennia of erosion, a great sea deposited the local building material: a sandstone that often harbors marine fossils. As the waters retreated, a series of ridges appeared along which we drive today, on roads named, variously, Center Ridge Road, Middle Ridge Road, North Ridge Road, and Murray Ridge Road.

I asked the farmers if I could see any of this material–I was eager for a rock from 150 feet below–but they explained that the drills pulverize beyond recognition whatever they pass through. All that remained were four very deep holes, in which they installed pipes through which liquid would circulate, bringing the fifty-five degree temperature one-hundred-fifty feet below the earth's surface up into our home. A heat pump inside the basement wall would take care of the rest, compressing the air until it reached the temperature to which we'd set our thermostat. (Mercifully, the process can be reversed on the hottest summer days: when we turn the thermostat to the cooling mode, the hot air travels back into the ground) Finally, the connection was made to our new hot water heater and furnace. "Furnace," however, seems a misnomer, because nothing burns inside it: no wood, coal, oil, or gas. It is really just the largest computer in our house, in charge of supervising the whole process. Tom, who is also a bee-keeper, celebrated the occasion by giving us a jar of his honey.

Although the initial expenditure was at least twice that of choosing a new gas furnace–the farmers were paid a set amount each well, for one thing–we had decided that this choice was our moral investment in the future. It turned out to be an investment in more ways than one. We undertook the project primarily as a way to decrease our ecological footprint; but very soon after the geothermal system was installed, natural gas prices began to rise, and they still are doing so. We have not taken the trouble to do the math, but our guess is that it won't be long before our investment in hope becomes profitable in dollars, as well. At first, the gas company did not know what to make of our new meter readings, and–despite the fact we had informed them about the change–sent us insistent notes throughout an entire year afterwards informing us that our infinitesimal bill from cooking with gas must be inaccurate.

The choice was also an investment in the future, as the nation moves towards an economy abundant in "green-collar" jobs, for we did provide some income for the farmers in their off-season. A recent bill signed into law as part of the energy bill authorizes $125 million a year to train people for these jobs. Twenty-percent of this money is dedicated to those who need the most support: the poor and unemployed, high-school dropouts, and formerly incarcerated people. Activist Van Jones, who helped advance the bill in Congress, calls it "green pathways out of poverty." He believes quite rightly that for the sustainable economy to be successful, it has to include everyone, not merely those who can afford the new technologies.

> We are seeing...a new image of an environmentalist with a hard hat, a lunch bucket, and rolled-up sleeves: somebody who says, 'Give us the tools. Give us the technology. We can fix America.' I believe this kind of working-class eco-populism will become the dominant political mode for progressives in the new century as we put people to work weatherizing buildings, installing solar panels, building windmills, and creating public transportation systems.[60]

The muddy eyesore that was our front yard was eventually leveled and replanted, so passing motorists no longer stopped to gape. But we still get lots of questions, "How do you like your geothermal? Is it warm enough?" We like it. We like to think that our home is now being heated in the winter, or cooled in the summer, mostly by Mother Earth, with only a small amount of electricity necessary to run the heat pumps or to give the geothermal system a boost in the coldest weather. We like the murmur of the heat pumps, the "swoosh" when it changes from one cycle to another, and the evenness of the heat. But most of all, we like the fact that it lessens our drain on the planet's resources, and expresses in a small way our philosophy of life, which is so well communicated on a grander scale in the Lewis Center a few blocks away.

We had no intention of being trail-blazers, but it turned out that ours was the first geothermal installation that Tom had done. Since then, the farmers, who receive much-needed new revenue for this labor, have been busy digging holes in other yards around town, contributing to the struggling rural economy. Our neighbors next door have built a new addition and installed geothermal heating and cooling for the entire house at the same time. Little did we think, when we made our decision, about the ripple effect.

That, I suppose, is what "witnessing"–defined as public affirmation by word or example, usually of religious faith or conviction–means. Especially when you set the example in a small town, where everybody is interested in your business!

Ponder and Pray

Is there an opportunity provided for a free energy audit in your community? It is the wisest first step you can take in assessing your energy use: the information you gain will contribute to the comfort of your home at the same time as it contributes to the health of the planet.

It is also a wise step for your church or place of business. When an audit was conducted for our local parish church, a building built over a century and a half ago, it was discovered that the heat from the struggling furnace in the basement below was exiting almost immediately through the poorly insulated roof.

Tending to our buildings like this is good stewardship, preserving their usefulness while conserving the limited resources of our planet.

4. Wheels

May the road rise to meet you.
May the wind always be at your back.
May the sun shine warm upon your face
May the rains fall softly upon your fields
until we meet again.

—Celtic Blessing[61]

My great-grandmother, Grandma Hascal, was born around the middle of the nineteenth century, but she still was very much alive when I was a little girl. What I remember most about her, aside from the fact that she was one of her grandchildren's best friends, is that she was afraid of cars.

It took a great deal of persuasion to get her to agree, when she was over ninety, to move to the East Coast to be near our family. After all, my father was going to bring her there in our family car.

Cars went too fast. They were new-fangled machines, and therefore unpredictable and dangerous. I do not believe that she ever really got used to them.

Maybe she was right to be afraid, for now we have an added reason for distrust of the internal combustion engine: automobiles have been responsible for incalculable environmental damage. Powered by fossil fuels, they deplete the planet's resources and spew pollutants into the air. The vast highway systems constructed on their behalf have set the stage for a sprawl that spreads its tentacles through farmland and forest. Their manufacture, their use, and their disposal are all problematic.

We can't go back to the days of my great-grandmother's girlhood, nor even to the childhood of my mother, who loved being met after school on snowy days by her father driving a sleigh pulled by the family horse. But there are some things we can do about the problem of cars.

We can choose alternatives. There is car-pooling, or innovative programs, like one in Philadelphia called Philly-CarShare that provides rental cars to its members for a nominal fee per hour. Recently, our small town has emulated Philadelphia's example by purchasing two automobiles for use by students and local residents. There is public transportation–or, if there is not, we can make our opinions known about the need for it. I have yet to figure out why it is that some people prefer huddling behind a wheel in heavy traffic to leaving the driving to someone else: a bus driver, perhaps, or the engineer of a commuter train or subway. I much prefer relaxing with a book, or with my thoughts, to being responsible for over a ton of steel on wheels.

For shorter trips, there is what my mother called "shank's mare," otherwise known as "my own two legs." Especially as we grow older, we are told that walking is the ideal weight-bearing exercise, helping us to build strong bones. It is especially useful if we have to actually go somewhere. Walking takes a bit of advanced planning for those who are accustomed to jumping in a car and traveling a few blocks in the blink of an eye, but it provides an opportunity to slow down our frantic inner metronome a few notches and to enjoy the scenery, while giving ourselves a workout totally free of charge. Maybe we'll even walk to the local fitness center and look in the window at treadmills being used by people who have driven the short distance from their homes in order to improve their cardiovascular capacity.

If you are impatient for a little more speed, there is my favorite mode of transportation, the bicycle. When I mount my vintage Raleigh, I am once again a child of seven or so, pedaling around and around the little circle at the end of our dead-end street. When I cycle to town, I do not need to find a parking space: there are ample slots in the bike racks on the sidewalk. To get there, I have not needed to confine my route to the streets, and could take short cuts through dormitory alleys and on campus sidewalks.

But when cars are necessary, what then? A few years ago, when our aging Honda Accord was slowly giving up the ghost, I spotted a friend getting into a new Civic hybrid outside the hardware store. It wasn't long before we road-tested her car on local streets, drove to the Honda dealer, and chose ours. Our friend and her husband have since added a new Toyota Prius to their stable, but we remain loyal to one of the first hybrid sedans produced in this country that is large enough to fit the needs of a one-car family.

It has become a kind of game for me to set the trip meter, which informs the driver about how many miles per gallon the car is achieving. A rather mesmerizing luminous blue gauge provides constant information about whether the car is being recharged by braking or steady driving (meter arrow to the left), coasting along on electricity (meter arrow absolutely vertical) or calling on the gasoline tank (meter arrow to the right). I've discovered that the secret to good mileage is gradual acceleration. On long trips through relatively flat country, we get well over fifty miles per gallon, and I can make it to the small metropolis eleven miles away on fifty-five mpg, if I do not have an impatient driver behind me at stop signs or traffic lights. I am not alone in getting a thrill from these numbers. The noted environmental writer Bill McKibben admits to the same obsession. "Does it sound like I pay inordinate attention to the gas gauge? Absolutely....When I'm behind the wheel, I'm an American—competitive, score-keeping, out to win. As I pull out of the driveway, what I think about is: can I beat my last trip? Will I make it home averaging sixty, or is the last hill on Route 125 going to knock me under? My Civic is only supposed to get fifty-two mpg, but I've got that beat cold."[62]

But both McKibben and I still use a small amount of gasoline, a fossil fuel, albeit a meager amount compared to most other cars in the parking lot. Some people, like a local entrepreneur in our town, use cooking oil, instead. The name of his product, which he makes available at a renovated service station, is "biodiesel," which gives little hint that its origin is really the left-over grease from local restaurants and grocery store delicatessens, its chemical structure altered to work in standard diesel engines. Another option is a car with two fuel tanks, one for straight vegetable oil–filtered to remove pieces of French Fries–and one for the diesel. And more new technologies are right down the road, so to speak.

By coincidence, the day I wrote this meditation, the television brought news that a major American automobile manufacturer had announced it was going to close fourteen factories in the next seven years, thereby causing about 30,000 people to lose their jobs. Interesting. The reason given was the fact that the public no longer wanted the SUVs and other gas-guzzling cars that were the manufacturer's specialty.

Ponder and Pray

You don't have to buy a hybrid-electric vehicle to decrease your toll on the planet. Instead, or as well, you can leave your car in the garage and get where you need to go in other ways.

Keep a log of the trips you make in your car during an entire week. At the end of the week, look over the log and notice whether or not you could have eliminated some of the driving by planning ahead and combining errands. Could you have taken public transportation, or shared a ride with someone else?

Take note of the distance you drove in each trip. Depending on where you live, you may realize that you could have walked or cycled in approximately the same time.

We are a mile away from the center of town and the college campus. When I estimate the time for driving, I must take into account the fact that I will not always be able to park near my destination. As a result, it takes almost the same amount of time to get there if I cycle, for I can park it in one of the many bicycle racks that grace our town. Walking takes longer, of course, but provides wonderful exercise and provides the entertainment of noticing houses, gardens, and people in a way that I miss when I make the trip just to get there as fast as possible.

Walking can also be a contemplative exercise. It reminds me of the concept of pilgrimage: a journey made to get to a sacred destination, but also in which the journeying itself is sacred. The next time you decide to take a walk, try using as a mantra the wonderful words of Thich Nhat Hanh, the Vietnamese monk and writer:

> *Walk and touch peace every moment.*
> *Walk and touch happiness every moment.*
> *Every step brings a fresh breeze.*
> *Each step makes a flower bloom.*
> *Kiss the Earth with your feet.*
> *Bring the Earth your love and happiness.*
> *The Earth will be safe when we feel safe in ourselves.*

Does connecting with the earth in this way make you expand your lungs and feel more fully alive? Does it feel as if you are connected to God, as well?

5. Bless This Food

As bread that was scattered on the hillside,
was gathered together and made one,
so too, we, your people,
scattered throughout the world,
are gathered around your table
and become one.

As grapes grown in the field
are gathered together and pressed into wine,
so too are we drawn together
and pressed by our times to share a common lot
and are transformed into your life-blood
for all.

—Adapted from The Didache, ca. 110[63]

"O God, bless this food to our use, and us to your love and service, and make us ever mindful of the needs of others. Amen." These are loaded words. In the process of expressing gratitude to the ultimate Source of all our nourishment, we are asking God also to make us uncomfortable. We're often told that our food choices affect our health. This prayer reminds us that our eating habits also affect the health of the world around us. At least three times a day, we make an impact on the planet for better or for worse. Michael Schut, former education director of Seattle's Earth

Ministry,[64] writes: "What we eat, where our food comes from, and how we eat are all expressions of our embeddedness in the fabric of creation and therefore an expression of our vision and our faith."[65]

Meals have so long been understood as more than simply the act of eating that it is relatively easy to make that connection. I used to attend the Passover meal at the synagogue, and every item on our plates helped us to "taste and see" the great events of the Exodus. The Christian Eucharist brings us the presence of "Christ our Passover" as we remember the supper Jesus shared with his disciples on the night before he was handed over to suffering and death. We gather with families or friends for holiday meals that have meaning far beyond the mere food on the table.

Food is also something over which most of us have some control. We can choose to eat responsibly, and we can also be grateful that we are in a position to do so, unlike some people across the world.

It is a shocking fact that 40,000 children die of hunger-related causes every *day*, while we in the United States have an epidemic of obesity. Being mindful of the needs of others involves responding to this knowledge. I find it interesting to observe ways in which my dinner plate has changed in my own lifetime. When I was a child, I sat down to dinner and saw before me three kinds of items, arranged neatly on my mother's china: meat, chicken or fish; potatoes or rice; and vegetables. When I began to cook for myself and my husband, my favorite cookbook was Peg Bracken's *The I*

Hate to Cook Book, which featured easy recipes that often included canned soup or other packaged food. When our sons were teenagers, another cookbook took its place on our kitchen shelf: *Diet for a Small Planet.*[66] It was the first time I had ever read that what we eat affects other people across the world. I began experimenting with some of the meatless recipes, and found them delicious. Our older son Christopher, a cross-country runner, read it as well. He resonated both to the text and to the recipes, which gave him more energy than a diet heavy in meat, and he became a vegetarian. He, along with my seminary friend Anita, who became a life-long vegetarian after visiting India and witnessing the hunger and poverty there, have responded radically to the inequity between those who are starving and those who have more than enough. But even a gesture in that direction helps: if Americans reduced meat consumption by as little as 10%, enough grain would be saved to feed 60 million people: it takes sixteen pounds of grain to produce one pound of beef, but only one pound of grain to make a pound of bread–the staff of life.

Ideally, I can best serve the planet's health if I have either grown the food in our garden or bought it at our local farmer's market or from the organic farm a mile away. By purchasing what is close at hand, I am not adding the environmental cost of transportation, which would increase the "carbon footprint" part of my footprint resume–my personal contribution to global warming. The CEO of the Tesco chain of supermarkets, based in Great Britain, intends to help guide conscientious consumers by placing airplane symbols on the packaging of those products that have been transported by air. In our country, produce travels an average of nearly fifteen hundred miles before it reaches our dinner plates, and about forty percent of our fruit comes from overseas. But the calculations can be complex: a study of the carbon cost of the global wine trade found that it is actually more "green" for New Yorkers to drink wine from Bordeaux, which is shipped by sea, than wine from California, sent by truck.[67] In Columbus, Ohio, not too far south of us, the wine from Bordeaux and from Napa have the same carbon intensity, good news for the oenophiles I know.

This part of a personal sustainability portfolio provides new delights. For I have learned that when I buy organic produce, meat, and dairy products raised through sustainable agricultural practices, the food is simply more delicious. I had discovered this fact quite early in life. My Grandmother Percy gardened organically because that is the way everybody did it then in rural East Smithfield, Pennsylvania. When we visited her in the summer, I loved to sneak a salt shaker out to the vegetable garden, sit down on the dirt, and pluck lettuce leaves. I would shake the salt on a leaf, pop it into my mouth, and savor the taste of ambrosia–the food of the gods. At home, I never had lettuce like that, because our lettuce came from the grocery store, probably after a long journey from California; it felt "dead" in comparison. Even today, eating a wonderful organic salad takes me right back to that experience of food full of life and flavor.

We can be mindful of the needs of others, also, by considering the practices that produced our food. Are we upset when we consider the plight of the peasants who are paid a pittance for the raising the coffee beans that make our coffee, and, in the process, are exposed to harmful herbicides and pesticides? Then we might consider coffee with the label "Fair Trade Organic" and know that, when we buy it, we can make a tremendous difference: coffee is the second largest commodity, after oil, that is traded in the global market. If we still enjoy meat, are we upset when we read about how the animals we consume are raised? We can seek out markets that carry free-range poultry, and also hope to find organic beef, lamb, and pork that have been raised with an understanding that these, too, are what the Buddhists call "sentient beings"–who, like us, can experience pain and fear.

Eating responsibly may cost a little more, but the alternative is mindless eating. Mindless eating has its costs, as well–to the health of the planet, society, and our own bodies. Mindful eating, on the other hand, can be a regular and grace-filled reminder of our being sustained by the entire web of life on earth. And, when we take the time to notice that, the food is more delicious, as well.

Ponder and Pray

Eat a meal mindfully, saying first this portion of a prayer similar to the one recited by the priest during the Eucharist:

"Blessed are you, God of all Creation; through your goodness we have this bread which earth has given and human hands have made...it will become for us the bread of life."

Focus on every bite you take, chewing it slowly and tasting it attentively. Everything in the meal is given you by the earth. Most of it has also come to you through the labor of other human beings, who have raised, harvested, transported, and often even prepared what you are eating. It becomes the bread of life, because, in essence, it *becomes* your own body: it provides your energy, builds your bones and muscles, and enhances your immune system. Meals provide the closest daily connection some people have with the earth, and, for all of us, meals can be times of blessing, gratitude, and pleasure.

6. Garbage

Composting teaches me that nothing in life is, in fact, "garbage." The way of nature is the way of use and reuse. When this lunchtime's carrot peeling is dumped on top of the seething compost pile, it enters into the slow process of becoming fertilizer for next summer's crop of carrots.

I learn, from observing nature's economy, that God intends me also to use all that I am given. I am meant to use my gifts and skills, my sorrows, and all the random happenings of life, spreading them out, as it were, in the fresh air of God to be transformed so that they can be life-giving, both for myself and the world around me.

—Nancy Roth, *Organic Prayer* [68]

If we were truly committed to ecological design, a chapter with the above title would be unnecessary. In nature, there is no garbage, as demonstrated by the natural cycles of life and death that we usually take for granted. Sometimes, however, they are brought dramatically to our attention.

Shortly before leaving for church one Ash Wednesday, my husband and I were startled by a thud against our kitchen door. We looked out just in time to see the end of a struggle, as a hawk rose from the ground with a female cardinal in its talons and flew to the top of the nearest pine to consume its prey. Our hearts were full of the sad memory of that encounter as we set off for the Ash Wednesday liturgy. When

I knelt at the altar rail and felt the rough cross traced on my forehead–"Remember you are dust, and to dust you shall return"–all I could think of was the cardinal. Then I turned my thoughts to the hawk; for him, the cardinal's death was life-giving, providing him with the energy to soar until he too returns to dust. Yes, nature is a skilled recycler, judging from the soil on a forest floor, or the magical transformation of the vegetable scraps and autumn leaves in our compost pile to nutrient-rich humus for our flower and vegetable beds. Nature never throws anything away.

But humans do, as any Martian would be able to tell us, for the Fresh Kills Landfill on Staten Island is one of the few human constructions that can be seen from space. Willard Gaylin writes, "I think...we're running out of out. *Out* is where my parents threw their garbage. You threw the garbage out. You can't throw the garbage *out* anymore. Out is where your children are going to live, where your grandchildren are going to live."[69]

Quite early in the environmental movement, the practice of recycling was a major sign that someone was serious about stewardship of the planet. In the past, institutions have sometimes been slow to adopt the practice, but things are changing rapidly in that regard. I am a faculty member of a program that meets regularly at various Episcopal retreat centers. At our meetings, the presenter on health always urges participants to drink lots of water, and cases of "pure spring water" in plastic bottles were provided to make the habit easy for us. When another faculty member

and I inquired about recycling the bottles at a certain retreat centers, we were told there were no recycling facili-
ties nearby. After a conference or two there, we had had it.
We discovered that we could take our empty bottles to our
rooms, stomp on them (which also had a therapeutic effect),
and shove them into our suitcases, so that we could recycle
them at home. I still wonder what they looked like when the
airlines x-rayed the luggage.

The institution that provides the program has solved the
problem now by providing participants with large refillable
canteens and investing in large water dispensers, so that no
longer do we need to save extra room in our luggage for the
purposes of recycling.

Most of us now live in localities that collect recyclable
materials. Each week, our town provides a pickup of recy-
clables. On the evening before the pickup, we take empty
plastic bottles, glass bottles, and metal cans, as well as piles
of newspapers and corrugated cardboard when we're sure
it's not going to rain. The next day, we hear the satisfying
cacophony of their being dumped into the special recycling
truck as we awaken in the morning. Local public schools are
raising money through placing recycling bins in their parking lots, and the newspapers, office paper, and magazines
that are left there are sold to raise money for school projects.
A couple times a year, the county collects batteries, paint,
turpentine, and other hazardous materials. I have discovered that the local retirement community has bins for plastic
bags and styrofoam peanuts. Goodwill, the Salvation Army,

and some local thrift shops accept cast-off clothing. Worn-out jeans go to the senior center, where they are woven into attractive throw rugs. We take magazines we've finished to the library's "free pile" or share them with neighbors, and take our egg cartons back to the natural foods store where we've bought the eggs. Yogurt containers go to the student food co-op for use as containers. But the most fun is the re-cycling chest we keep in our basement for the benefit of the local early childhood center. There I toss "treasures": scraps of gift wrap and ribbons, fluffy balls of cotton from the tops of medicine bottles, plastic bottle tops, odd styrofoam forms that once protected electronic equipment during shipping, feathers, bits of fabric, and flower catalogs. Every once in a while I sort the contents of the chest, and set off for the center with the booty. I am greeted with enthusiasm each time, for these objects become the raw material for some imaginative art on the part of the students.

Pre-cycling, which means avoiding overpackaging in the first place, also contributes to diminishing our garbage. When we have a choice, we try to buy minimally packaged items. I like the student food co-op because I can buy in bulk and take home staples like rice and oatmeal in my own con-tainers. We try to avoid disposable items. When the check-out clerk at the grocery store asks, "paper or plastic?" I answer, "I have my own bags," and lift my canvas bag col-lection out of the shopping cart.

All of this has become habitual, no trouble at all, and slowly but surely, it is becoming habitual for most of us, as well as for our institutions. I do have to admit, however, that it was especially easy for me, because the practice had never seemed "new." I am dating myself by admitting the thrill I got as a child while rolling discarded tin foil into an ever-larger ball, "for the war effort." My mother and father, having lived through the Depression, were by nature thrifty, so it is in my genes.

One of my seminary professors was fond of going on "digs" in the Holy Land. He had made a bas-relief of sorts that was mounted on the classroom wall, a kind of vertical "slice" that was a replica of his archaeological efforts. We could see the layers of civilization in the form of shards of pottery or fragments of a building. They helped us imagine what it might have been like to live in biblical times.

I've sometimes wondered what will our descendants would think should they embark on similar ventures many centuries hence? My guess is that they will be appalled, as they look at all the detritus of our society: "What an odd society they were, to create such a mess!"

Ponder and Pray

If you feel brave, conduct a census of your garbage can–or (if you are squeamish) make a list of what you throw into it during the course of 24 hours. Is there any way you can diminish the amount of garbage?

Have you thought about your emotional "garbage," as well–those regrets, sorrows, and resentments buried deep in your soul? Expose this garbage to the light and allow God to transform it, like compost, into something that enriches your spirit and your life.

7. TURNING OFF THE LIGHTS

*For God loves nothing so much as the person who lives with
wisdom.*
*She is more beautiful than the sun, and excels every constella-
tion of the stars.*
Compared with the light she is found to be superior,
*for it is succeeded by the night, but against wisdom evil does
not prevail.*
She reaches mightily from one end of the earth to the other,
and she orders all things well.

—The Wisdom of Solomon 7:28-8:1

"Have you written anything yet about turning off
lights?" asked my husband. He and I were both raised by
parents who used the words, "Remember to turn off the
lights," like a litany. His question was not only about lights,
of course, but about the practice of conservation. The good
news is that we do not need to buy shiny new furnaces, dig
holes for geothermal wells, or buy a fuel-efficient car in order to make a difference. We can simply turn off the lights
when we are not using them, and save energy in myriad
other quite simple ways. We might be more motivated if a
monitor providing constant feedback about energy use were
prominently placed in each home, as it is in the lobby of
the Adam J. Lewis Center for Environmental Studies. Or
perhaps we could have a neighborhood competition about
who could consume the least energy in a given month, the

way certain dormitories here on campus have done. The students also monitored water use, and took shorter showers–a extraordinary sacrifice, if my memory serves me correctly, for people of that age.

Innumerable books have been written in the last couple of decades about ways to "save the earth" through "fifty simple things" or "one hundred ways" or "two minutes a day," and I cannot begin to list them all. But this book would not be complete if I did not suggest a few.

Can one person alone "save the earth" by following even fifty, or a hundred, of these suggestions? Probably not. The power lies in the fact that, cumulatively, individual actions make a difference. They also can become spiritual practices that continue to remind us of our connection with creation and express our care for it in very practical ways. Just as our prayer can become habitual prayer through the habit of recognizing God's presence throughout the day, these practices can become habitual actions. When we first do some of these prayers-in-action, they may seem difficult, time-consuming, or a bother. As we continue to do them, they become a seamless part of our routine. More than that, they begin to feel sacramental, because they are an outward sign of our love.

Some, like the lights, come under the category of energy use. If we have a standard furnace, we can turn down the thermostat at night, and perhaps even put on an extra sweater during the day in order to lower the heat by a notch or so. In the summer, we can go easy on the air-conditioning by turning up the thermostat, or by foregoing air conditioning altogether and simply opening the windows to let in some fresh breezes. I am amazed how one's body can become accustomed to certain temperatures. Because of the low thermostat settings in the South during the summer months, I always pack a warm sweater when I travel in that direction in the summer. Although I am a Yankee and can deal with cold air during the winter, in the summer those frigid southern interiors tend to give me goosebumps.

We can use solar power for drying clothes. Sound complicated? All it takes is some clothes pins, an "umbrella" clothesline, or a length of clothesline and tree or two. The smell of sheets dried in the sunshine lulled me to sleep throughout my childhood. I remember overhearing my mother and the woman next door discussing over the back fence the delights of hanging out the clothes, even as other women in the neighborhood were buying electric dryers. "There is nothing like the fresh smell," they said, "and besides, I like to stand out here in the sunshine, talking to you!" It was a different era, of course, and perhaps we do not always have the time, the space, or the weather conditions, to hang clothes outdoors. But when we do, it can be both a leisurely moment to enjoy nature and a tremendous savings, for a clothes dryer is one of the most greedy consumers of energy in our home. For that matter–although they do not provide quite as much pleasure–indoor clotheslines like the ones strung in our basement are another way to conserve energy.

As I wrote earlier, we can educate ourselves about the products we use to clean our homes. For a very short time many years ago, we hired someone to clean our house occasionally. One day I returned home, walked in the front door, and found that I could hardly breathe: she had used a product on the vinyl in our front hall that had interacted with the petrochemicals in the vinyl and produced something dreadfully toxic, to judge by its foul smell. (To give her credit, she was trying to eradicate the marks made by the tires of the bikes we parked there.) Potentially toxic chemicals lurk in most commercial cleaning products; they are designed to get a job done quickly but almost never gently or safely, and almost all of them have the words "danger," "warning," and "caution" on their labels.

There are alternative products, most of which are probably already in your kitchen cabinets. Some of them may require some elbow grease, but the next time you go to the gym, you will probably discover that your arm strength has increased–and you've accomplished something besides. Your home will be clean, and you will have moved one more step toward making it a synthetic-chemical-free zone!

Should your home be surrounded by lawn and garden, you'll have plenty of books to choose from to educate you about safe and sustainable gardening. My favorite happens to be a book of gardening advice written in the style of Beatles lyrics,[70] but, if that is not your style, you can learn about organic gardening from more formal presentations. Organic gardening is a prime example of respecting ecological design through working with, rather than against, nature. The biotic life of the soil is maintained, pest management is approached through imitating the way nature works, and fertility is increased through using compost and cover crops rather than quick-fix synthetic chemicals. It is very satisfying to garden in this way, a fact that I have celebrated in my own book, *Organic Prayer*.

"Have you written anything yet about turning off the lights"? I realize I have neglected to write anything about compact fluorescent light bulbs, which use only a quarter of the energy needed by incandescent bulbs. They are becoming more readily available and, although they cost more in the beginning, they last up to ten times longer than incandescent bulbs. Last summer, our grass-roots environmental group made them available to the community, and I bought enough for every fixture in the house that could use them. Some of them are still waiting for me to get "harps" for those lampshades that clip onto bulbs, since I can't imagine how a spiraling fluorescent bulb could endure such a thing. But even when the time comes that we can honestly call our house incandescent-free, I will hear the voice of my mother: "Remember to turn off the lights."

Ponder and Pray

Try to replace with compact fluorescent bulbs as many incandescent lights as you are able, and compare your electrical bills for the months before and the months after you have done so. You have saved money, of course, but you have also made an effort to contribute to Earth's healing. Converting to more sustainable lighting is only one of many ideas to help you tend your household with the wisdom mentioned in the quotation that preceded this chapter: "For God loves nothing so much as the person who lives with wisdom. She is more beautiful than the sun...."

Find a source for other ideas, whether online, or in a book. Do not try to do everything at once; it is less daunting to choose one idea a week, or two a month. Slowly but surely, these will become a habitual part of your life, "reaching mightily from one end of your [home] to the other," and all things will be "ordered well"!

8. Speaking Out

But Moses said to the Lord, "O my Lord, I have never been eloquent, neither in the past nor even now that you have spoken to your servant; but I am slow of speech and slow of tongue." Then the Lord said to him, "Who gives speech to mortals? Who makes them mute or deaf, seeing or blind? Is it not I, the Lord? Now go, and I will be with your mouth and teach you what you are to speak."

—Exodus 4:10-12

Soon after we moved to Oberlin–a small town that many would consider fairly idyllic, despite some pockets of poverty and the usual problems that face any community in which real human beings live–an alarming article appeared in the local newspaper. It told of a plan by the county commissioners to enlarge a small local airport, used mostly by private recreational planes, that lay just two miles north of town. The runways were to be extended so that large cargo jets could land, and there were reports that there was already interest on the part of a Russian entrepreneur who wanted to export motorcycles and vodka to northern Ohio. The project invited sprawl, pollution, and increased noise, to the detriment of a rural countryside, and was driven by what experts would eventually tell us was the vain hope of economic growth. Besides, Cleveland Hopkins Airport is only a half hour distant.

After I read the article, I reacted by writing to the head county commissioner on my personal stationery, telling him about my concerns. I spoke about the reasons we had decided to move here, which included a quiet town, a college with a conservatory of music, and a peaceful rural landscape. I wrote also about the need for wisdom and long-range planning in any development that would bring congestion, pollution, and noise to the surrounding region. Two days later, the commissioner's office telephoned and invited me to meet with the commissioner "to talk–and to bring along some friends, if I wished." I invited David Orr, two Oberlin city council members, and a commissioner in the township in which the airport was located. The last was amazed when I called him, for he had been trying to get the commissioner's ear for weeks, and had been ignored.

On the appointed day, the five of us arrived for our meeting, and the county commissioner's jaw dropped when we walked in the door. I had brought along all the people he had been avoiding! During the next half hour or so, we did our best to educate him about the issues, although he remained unconvinced. This meeting was the beginning of a flurry of political involvement that included many gatherings of a grass roots organization. The group helped to plan county-wide informational meetings for the public, and went door-to-door to the airport's neighbors, who were horrified at the prospect of the development and insulted that their opinions on the matter had not been taken into consideration. The project as it stood was finally dropped, due to public resistance and economic constraints.

I suspect that the key to the very *beginning* of the story–the fact that I gained an audience with the commissioner while others did not–is found in the letterhead on my personal stationery. It reads, "*The Rev.* Nancy Roth." Apparently, the commissioner, who never could be persuaded to meet with the other political figures, was either intimidated or intrigued by that title "The Rev." Little did he suspect who that "Reverend's" friends would be.

The event gave me a taste of how it felt to confront "authority" by saying, "This is wrong." It is not a task to which I come easily, for I prefer reconciliation and compromise rather than confrontation, but I have to admit that the challenge was exhilarating. I cannot say whether our accomplishment was significant, or even enduring, but we had forestalled the unwise development for the time being, and also inspired some land-use planning that has already served our area well.

In November of 2006, a similar grass roots group formed here after viewing Al Gore's documentary *An Inconvenient Truth* at a local church. Because the group comes mainly from the faith communities in town, it is called ICE: the Interfaith Committee on the Environment. Its function is "think globally and act locally": to educate, and to communicate. It was formed in the nick of time, for soon our local power company was faced with a decision about whether to invest in a so-called "clean coal" plant in the southern part of our state. It would be a fifty-year obligation. ICE swung into action and gathered facts and figures which were shared with the city council and the power company, as well as the general public. Everyone involved wanted to do the right thing, but the issue was extremely complicated. Would there be an extra burden on the poor in our community if we *did* not agree to buy in to the coal plant? On the other hand, would we be burdened with horrendous expenses in the future if we *did,* because of expected regulations and carbon taxes (these are believed by many to be one of the best hopes for our global future) by the federal government? Was coal even going to be an option for generating power fifty years hence, or would it be a thing of the distant past by then? How much could our decision about the plant affect the environmental and social consequences of mountaintop removal in West Virginia for the purposes of coal mining? How would it affect the quality of life in the southern Ohio where the plant was to be built? Last but not least, how would the decision affect our descendants, and what would they think of our decision when they looked back at us over history?

The final meeting on the subject took place just as I was putting the finishing touches on this book. It was an amazing example of democracy in action: everyone who wished to speak had a say, and all were listened to with respect. All angles were considered, including my thoughts about "choosing life": in my role as clergy, I took the liberty of quoting Deuteronomy, "Choose life."

The work that ICE had done in gathering facts and

figures, the varied testimonies of residents, and a fine presentation by a representative from the Natural Resources Defense Council, all made a tremendous difference, for the end result was that the city council had the courage to turn down the invitation to subsidize the coal plant. Our officials will now explore other options as Oberlin tries to build up its sustainable energy portfolio: a proportion of our power already comes from hydroelectric plants, wind farms, and methane gas from a nearby landfill.

The outcome could have been otherwise: the vote was four to three. But people spoke out, even some who are not accustomed to doing so, and the hard facts turned out to be undeniable.

One does not always need to appear in person to make one's opinion known, however. The internet gives us many opportunities to speak our minds to those in power. There are many sites, both religious and secular, that appear on my computer screen to inform me about the ways I can contribute to a just society. Sometimes they ask me to telephone or write a letter to my senators and representatives. Sometimes I need to access a website and follow the instructions, although I must confess that, given the amount of e-mail on the screen, my favorite messages require me just to click to be counted as a signatory on the petition, while adding my own words if I wish.

It almost goes without saying that we have another, even more powerful, means of speaking out. That is when we enter a voting booth to cast our ballot. This incredible privilege and responsibility is never to be taken for granted. The students here did not take it for granted in the 2004 presidential election. Because of the shortage of voting machines, many of them stood in the rain for the greater part of the day in order to make their will known. The curtained booth is, in fact, sacred space, like a confessional. In it we do, in fact, confess–in the sense of making known–our values, our hopes, and our dreams, for a better world.

Our beliefs are revealed through our action, as the prophet Amos reminded those who left behind their faith when they exited the temple. He reminds us as well.

> I hate, I despise your festivals;
> and I take no delight in your solemn assemblies...
> Take away from me the noise of your songs;
> I will not listen to the melody of your harps.
> But let justice roll down like waters,
> and righteousness like an everflowing stream.
> (Amos 5:21, 23-4.)

Ponder and Pray

There are many web sites, both denominational and secular, that can inform us about the current important justice issues about which we need to speak out. The Episcopal Church, for example, provides an e-mail "alert" service through the Episcopal Public Policy Network: www.episcopalchurch.org/eppn. They also will mail you a *Capitol Hill Directory* of your representatives and senators. It is likely that other denominations have similar web sites. You can also google "environmental organizations," and subscribe to an e-mail "alert" of your liking.

There is nothing, however, like speaking out in person. One of the speakers the night of the coal plant decision was a woman who lives in local subsidized housing. One of the talking points of those in the room who wanted to buy in to the coal plant was that we had to make sure there was ample cheap coal power on account of those in this community who could not afford to pay more. This woman stood up, identified herself as one of these, and continued by saying that this assumption about those who live in poverty was wrong, and that she had decided to speak out against the plant, although she had been very shy about doing so. She made a tremendous impact.

If you have an opinion and are reluctant to speak out—whether it be through appearing in a town meeting, through writing a letter to the editor of your local paper, or telephoning or writing to your representatives in Congress—know that you are not alone. It is those who do not find it easy to express themselves publicly who often are heard with most interest. Take courage from the example in Exodus that begins this chapter!

HOPE

The singers and the dancers will say,
"All my fresh springs are in you."

—Psalm 87:7

Our hearts and spirits need to be nourished throughout this journey. Our final chapters will suggest a few of the resources that can inspire and support us. We will discover that this venture is not new, but that we stand as part of a long lineage of prophets, saints, mystics, and theologians who understand God's deep passion and care for creation. We will pay homage to those Celtic peoples who were so attuned to daily life that every action was lifted to God in prayer. A painter and a composer will serve as examples of the way the arts can inspire, enlighten, and strengthen us. We'll cast our eyes upon those beacons of hope for the future: our children. We will discover ways of praying that include the new and pressing issues facing the planet. Finally, we will dance, in movements that symbolize our search for the "place that's right," as we seek to contribute to a world that will be once again a valley of love and of delight.

1. A Cloud of Witnesses

Therefore we praise you, joining our voices with Angels and
Archangels and with all the company of heaven, who for ever
sing this hymn to proclaim the glory of your Name:
Holy, holy, holy Lord, God of power and might,
heaven and earth are full of your glory.

—*The Holy Eucharist, Rite Two,*
The Book of Common Prayer

We are not on this journey alone; there are many voices
that support us. We have allies not only in the biblical tradition, but in generations of saints, monastics, and theologians who have expressed a deep connection with nature
in their own time. We also are joined by those who, in our
own era, are calling humanity to a new paradigm and to a
manner of life that expresses this vision. Their words could
fill an extensive anthology, but we can at least make the
acquaintance of a few of these companions in the confines
of these pages. We will begin with a whirlwind overview of
the biblical references to nature, a subject that could fill, and
has filled, more than one book.

Certainly the creation stories in Genesis give us insight
into the understandings of their inventors. We have already
spoken of the earliest creation story, found in the second
chapter of Genesis. Genesis 1 contains (counter-intuitive-
ly) a later story, in which God creates everything *else*–sky,

oceans, plants, trees, sun, moon, fish, birds, and creeping things–before deciding to make humankind in the divine image. In the Hebrew story, the greater part of the first six "days" of creation was given to preparing the environment in which humanity was to live and multiply. Although the descendants of the first "earthlings" are eventually warned not to fall prey to the seduction of worshiping as gods the various aspects of nature, the Hebrew prayer book–the Psalter–always takes for granted that the heavens declare God's glory and that the firmament proclaims God's handiwork:[71]

> *Praise God, sun and moon; sing praise, all you shining stars...*
> *Praise God from the earth, you sea-monsters and all deeps;*
> *Fire and hail, snow and fog, tempestuous wind, doing God's will;*
> *Mountains and all hills, fruit trees and all cedars;*
> *Wild beasts and all cattle, creeping things and winged birds....*
> *Let them praise your Name, O God, for your Name only is exalted;*
> *your splendor is over earth and heaven.*[72]

We have already spoken of God's great speech out of the whirlwind beginning in Chapter 38 of the Book of Job: an invitation, if there ever was one, to human humility. It is summed up in one question: "Job, could you have made all this?" Then there is the Song of Solomon; no doubt you have attended weddings where you have heard parts of this most earthy book of the Bible, which possibly originated as a collection of songs actually used for Hebrew weddings.

Thanks to the fact that both the Jewish and Christian traditions found another level of meaning in the work–the love between God and God's people–we can open our Bibles and find pleasure in lines such as the following:

Arise, my love, my fair one, and come away;
for now the winter is past, the rain is over and gone.
The flowers appear on the earth;
the time of singing has come,
and the voice of the turtledove is heard in our land.
The fig tree puts forth its figs,
and the vines are in blossom;
they give forth fragrance.
(Song of Solomon: 2:10b-13.)

For timely guidance about environmental justice, we can look to the prophets:

Ah, you who join house to house, who add field to field until there is room for no one but you, and you are left to live alone in the midst of the land! (Is.5:8) The earth dries up and withers, the world languishes and withers; the heavens languish together with the earth. The earth lies polluted under its inhabitants.... (Is. 24: 4-5) Is it not enough for you to feed on the good pasture, but you must tread down with your feet the rest of your pasture? When you drink of clear water, must you foul the rest with your feet? (Ez.34:18)

To reach his listeners in the agricultural milieu of the first century, it is natural that Jesus used analogies from the natural world:..."the tree is known by its fruit" (Matt. 12:33); "The kingdom of heaven is compared to someone who sowed good seed in his field...."(Matt. 13:24); "The earth produces of itself, first the stalk, then the head, then the full grain in the head" (Mark 4:28); "With what can we compare the kingdom of God?....It is like a mustard seed...." (Mark 4:31); "Which one of you, having a hundred sheep and losing one of them, does not leave the ninety-nine in the wilderness and go after the one that is lost until he finds it?"(Luke 15:3); "I am the true vine, and my Father is the vinegrower." (John 15:1).

When Christianity became more and more intertwined with the culture after the conversion of Constantine, people who sought a more muscular faith began to flee to the desert. What they sought can inform us, as well, as we seek to live in harmony with God, earth, and neighbor: "This struggle 'that my heart may be pure to all'" (in the words of Amma Sarah) "is based on the new life the person has chosen rather than an exterior obligation. The desire for moral behavior is internal...."[73] The subsequent development of monastic communities produced vows (such as stability and conversion of life, or poverty, chastity, and obedience) that underscored the desire to live with simplicity, free from the pressures and expectations of the surrounding culture.

St. Francis of Assisi (d. 1226), founder of the Franciscans, is generally claimed as the patron saint of environmentalists, but the legends about his taming of the wolf of Gubbio and preaching to the birds, and his Canticle of the Sun

("All praise be yours, my Lord, with all your creatures...."),
are only the tip of the iceberg. What lay underneath the surface was Francis's sense of being "wedded" to Lady Poverty;
he forsook material possessions and comfort for the sake
of God and the world–including lepers and creatures both
furred and feathered.

In the previous century, Hildegard of Bingen (1098-
1179)–abbess, musician, composer, poet, scientist, and
mystic–had tried to express a similar sense of God in nature through a word she coined: *viriditas,* which meant the
"power for green growth" given by the Spirit. In her hymn
to Mary, she writes: "Hail to you, O greenest, most fertile
branch!"[74] Her compatriot Meister Eckhart (1260-1329)
was to write the words I quoted at the beginning of an earlier chapter of this book: "Every single creature is full of
God and is a book about God....If I spent enough time with
the tiniest creature–even a caterpillar–I would never have to
prepare a sermon."[75]

Across the English Channel, Dame Julian of Norwich
(1324-c.1417), a visionary who lived her vowed life in the
seclusion of a cell, was to write about seeing in a hazelnut
"everything that was made," and understanding that God
made it, loves it, and preserves it.

The voices of these mystics of the church support the
contention that prayer is to theology as original research
is to science. The direct experience of the holy articulated
by the mystics through word, art, or action, is, in a sense,
"organized" by the theologians who think in a more linear

manner. When I walked into Systematic Theology class for the first time, I was amazed to hear the professor say, "This will be the most practical course in your whole seminary career." A quarter of a century later, I would remember those words when Professor David Orr spoke of the power of the ideas which guide us as we live our lives. Just as theological concepts are the foundation for the way the seminary students would one day carry out their pastoral and liturgical duties, so ideas shape the way that all human beings relate to others of our species or to the natural world.

Systematic thinkers help us articulate and reflect on our experience. Two theologians in particular have done that for me. One is Jürgen Moltman, whom I heard at a conference in the 1980's; he recasts theology in the light of modern natural science and of environmental concerns. About the same time, at a memorable conference on the shore of Long Island Sound, I was privileged to sit at the feet of the Roman Catholic theologian Thomas Berry, about whom I have written earlier in this book. Each year, I discover more theologians who share their wisdom about how to *think* about our relationship with the creation.

We are not alone. We are surrounded by a cloud of witnesses like the ones I have named, and also by innumerable others. One of the best ways we can feed our souls and gather courage at the same time is to get to know them.

Ponder and Pray

The contemporary theologian Sally McFague is a companion worth getting to know. She takes an old idea–that all creation is a revelation of God–and gives it new meaning in the light of our behavior toward the physical world:

> The world is our meeting place with God...as the
> body of God, it is wondrously, awesomely, divinely
> mysterious....[This essay] focuses on embodiment, inviting
> us to do something that Christians have seldom done: think
> about God and bodies. What would it mean, for instance,
> to share the basic necessities of survival with other bodies?
> To see Jesus of Nazareth as paradigmatic of God's love for
> bodies? To interpret creation as all the myriad forms of mat-
> ter bodied forth from God and empowered with the breath
> of life, the spirit of God? To consider ourselves as inspirited
> bodies profoundly interrelated with all other such bodies
> and yet having the special distinction of shared responsibil-
> ity with God for the well-being of our planet? Such a focus
> causes us to see differently, to see dimensions of the relation
> of God and the world that we have not seen before.[76]

Take some time to notice your own "embodiment"–your weight (your *adamah*) and your breath (the gift of God's *ruach*). Become aware of God's presence with you, then read the passage above again, very slowly, taking as much time as you wish in between sentences to let the words reverberate in your spirit. Take at least ten minutes with this meditation.

Afterwards, if you wish, jot down some thoughts or phrases that have come to you as a result.

2. Celts

Almighty God, Creator
the morning is yours, rising into fullness.
The summer is yours, dipping into autumn.
Eternity is yours, dipping into time.
The vibrant grasses, the scent of flowers,
the lichen on the rocks, the tang of seaweed. All is yours.
Gladly we live in this garden of your creating.

—*Celtic Prayer*[77]

You have to really *want* to go there to make the pilgrimage to Iona. Your journey to this remote little island in the Inner Hebrides off the west coast of Scotland usually begins in Glasgow, and first requires that you make your way, by train, bus, or car, to Oban, where you might decide to spend the night in a bed and breakfast in order to take the early ferry to Mull, an island that could well have provided the scenery for *Lord of the Rings*. Once there, you will board a local bus and cross Mull; and, soon after you pass through the little village of Bunessan (a village after which the haunting melody for "Morning Has Broken" was named), you board a small ferry for the short passage across the blue-green Sound of Mull. If you are staying at Bishop's House–a grey stone retreat center–as I did on my first visit to Iona, you will walk up the main street, passing the Argyll Hotel, a pottery, a silversmith, and a house with a poster offering boat rides to the Island of

Staffa, which is the site of the famous Fingal's Cave and the home, depending on the season, of colonies of puffins. Once you have left your luggage at Bishop's House, a member of its staff will point out the path to your destination: Iona Abbey. You will need to watch your step as you walk there, for you will be making your way through the flock of sheep grazing in the pastures between the abbey and the beach. You pass the ruins of a monastic chapel and walk between a stone wall and the abbey—a twentieth-century restoration built on the ruins of the Benedictine foundation built around 1200. As you walk beyond the west front of the abbey, there suddenly looms over you something much more ancient. It dates from the eighth century: a high stone cross, a single circle surrounding its center, in the manner of Celtic crosses.

You walk around it and notice that there are bas-reliefs carved on both sides. As you face the abbey, those scenes are biblical: the Virgin and child, Daniel flanked by lions, Abraham and Isaac, David playing his harp and encountering Goliath. But as you walk around to the other side—the one that faces the blue-green sea and the pasture full of sheep—you enter another world. There, you see, carved in heavy relief, the world of nature, with patterns of round bosses encircled by serpents and, at the top, lion-like creatures. The cross is a sermon in stone whose theme is both the world of the sacred story and the world of creation, embraced by a central circle. This cross, known as the Cross of St. Martin, expresses the essence of what is known as "Celtic Spirituality": our heritage from the Christian tradition that first flourished in Ireland and then was brought to Iona by the monk Columba, who landed there on a pebbled beach at the far end of the island.

At the Synod of Whitby, sixty-seven years after Columba's death, the English church chose to adopt the rites, customs, and calendar of an alternative version of the faith brought by the missionary Augustine of Canterbury, who had landed in Canterbury the same year that Columba came to Scotland. However, the Celtic spirit was never truly extinguished. It is preserved visually in some of the great works of art of Western civilization: the Book of Kells, the Lindisfarne Gospels, the Ardagh Chalice, numerous carvings on small country churches, and standing crosses like the ones on Iona. Moreover, thanks to the mission of a man named Alexander Carmichael, who wandered the Western Highlands for much of the second half of the nineteenth century collecting hundreds of prayers from the humble people who lived there, we have a treasure-trove of poetry and prayer that preserves the spirit of the Celtic tradition.

Reading the chants and incantations of the peasants, we learn that in every moment of daily life, all things were intertwined, like the illuminations of the Book of Kells:

> The monk who was responsible for the opening of St. John's Gospel...winds spirals with a thread that almost becomes invisible and keeps the interconnecting lines going....He brings into his canvas all the familiar figures, the vines and the spirals, the elongated animals and birds, and in particular his favourite ribbon-shaped snakes."[78]

For the cottagers who shared their incantations with Carmichael, the intertwining of spirit and matter was not an abstract idea, but an experience. Those who chanted these prayers felt the presence of the Trinity, along with Mary the mother of Jesus, the angelic host, and St. Bridget and the other saints, hovering over them, surrounding them, and blessing them like the very air that they breathed as they went about their daily work.

A woman would begin her day by kindling her fire "in the presence of the holy angels of heaven," and splash her face with three palmfuls of water in the name of the Trinity.

She would milk her cow in the presence of the saints:

"Come, Mary, and milk my cow,
Come, Bride [Bridget], and encompass her,
Come, Columba the benign,
And twine thine arm around my cow."

In the meantime, her husband would set forth to work in the fields: "Bless to me, O God, The earth beneath my foot...."

He put his herd into the safekeeping of Mary, the saints, and the angels:

"Closed to you be every pit
Smooth to you be every hill,
Snug to you be every bare spot,
Beside the cold mountains...

The fellowship of Michael victorious be yours,
In nibbling, in chewing, in munching."

When the grain was ripe for harvest, he would cut a sheaf and circle it around his head as he chanted, "God bless Thou thyself my reaping, Each ear and handful in the sheaf."

When he set out for sea, he would pray, "Bless our boatmen and our boat, Bless our anchors and our oars, Each stay and halyard and traveller, Our mainsails to our tall masts."[79]

George McLeod, the founder of the present-day Iona Community, an ecumenical community whose members express the Celtic spirit through the Christian activism that issues from their own sense of God-in-the-world, was once asked why he thought it was so urgent that people should rediscover the Celtic tradition:

"Everyone today keeps asking, 'What is the Matter?'... and the short answer is MATTER is the matter. It is our view of matter, the extent to which the church has spiritualized the faith and set it apart from the material world, that has brought us where we are today."[80]

MATTER is the matter. This legacy of our Celtic ancestors both enriches our spirit and illumines our minds. It tells us that Matter matters, and that we are inextricably intertwined with the natural world that supports, protects, and nourishes us, because it is filled with God.

Ponder and Pray

I have told the story many times of a dinner party I hosted soon after my first trip to Iona. The guests left late, and there were many dishes. As I stood before the sink feeling depressed, it occurred to me to imagine myself a Celtic housewife, faced with this task. I would pray. So I prayed, "O Holy Trinity, St. Mary and St. Bridget, Archangel Michael, and all the hosts of heaven, look down and bless these pots and pans." My spirits lifted, my energy was restored, and I found myself smiling.

All things were material for prayer in the lives of Celtic peoples, since they knew the world was full of God's presence. We can follow their example: whatever our state of mind, the simple act of acknowledging the divine presence in creation and in all our activities can transform our lives.

Do you have a concern, especially about the plight of the planet, that weighs you down? If you were a Celtic farmer or housewife, how would you pray about it? Compose an incantation of your own, and perhaps even begin a series of such prayers in a journal.

3. Art

O God, whom saints and angels delight to worship in heaven:
Be ever present with your servants who seek through art and
music
to perfect the praises offered by your people on earth;
and grant to them even now glimpses of your beauty,
and make them worthy at length to behold it unveiled for
evermore;
through Jesus Christ our Lord. Amen.

—*The Book of Common Prayer* [81]

When I was asked to lead a retreat in Santa Fe, New Mexico, my heart leapt, for finally I would be able to see Georgia O'Keefe country. O'Keefe, the artist who is known both through her paintings and through the photography of her husband and mentor Alfred Steiglitz, lived in nearby Abiquiu in her later years, until her death in 1986 at the age of 98.

I arrived a day before the retreat was to begin, so that I could make an unhurried visit to the O'Keefe Museum. It is located a block or so off Santa Fe's picturesque Plaza, which is bordered on one side by the venerable Palace of the Governors. The portico of the palace, a long adobe structure, protects the many Native American jewelry-makers who sit there during the day beside the colorful blankets on which they have spread out their wares. As I passed along the portico on the way to the museum, my eyes fell upon a pair of earrings from which dangled small silver images of Kokopelli, a puckish figure bent forward in a dance, playing his flute. Despite his youthful energy, Kokopelli is probably almost three thousand years old, judging from petroglyphs and pottery found throughout the Southwest. He is the symbol of fertility for all life; his invisible presence is said to be felt whenever life comes forth from seed, whether the seed be that of plants or animals.

I bought the earrings. As a dancer and musician, I love the concept of music and dance bringing growth and fertility to the earth. As I continued on to the O'Keefe Museum, I thought about the ways that the arts have helped open my own eyes to the beauty and abundance of the natural world around me.

My visit there was one of those times that a museum was transformed into sacred space. Some of what I heard on my rented audioguide helped me discover why that was so.

I had always been attracted to O'Keefe's paintings, for her art flowed directly from her powerful experience of nature. As I gazed at a painting of the spiraling petals of the "Abstraction on White Rose" (1927), the audiotape described the rose, spiraling inwards from its vortex, as an expression of the "life force, energy, and power of the invisible." As the viewer looks at the rose, she contemplates also O'Keefe's internal state. Her painting invites us to experience that internal state ourselves, just as we might while watching a drama on the stage, for example.

Looking at "Bear Lake, New Mexico" (1930), I learned that O'Keefe loved trees, as I also do. Perhaps she found that they were kindred spirits: a tree draws nourishment from the earth and grows tall, becoming a living force within the world.

I stood before "Black Hollyhock, Blue Larkspur" (1930), which depicts the flowers at their vibrant prime. There, as I looked at a large black hollyhock blossom beside which the larkspur seemed to "move back and forth as if in performance," I heard the now familiar voice on the audioguide tell me that "O'Keefe's studies of natural forms, such as flowers, heighten our awareness of the forms when we next see them in nature. After that, should we come back to look at the painting, we experience it with more complexity."

When I finally exited the museum, I sat down on a patio chair near the front door and called my friend Susan, a painter and monastic, whose work vibrates with a similar spirit. As I told her about the exhibit, she said, "These are icons!" Indeed, like the sacred images of Orthodox Christianity, O'Keefe's paintings are *windows*. They invite us to see deeply beyond their surface into the "is-ness" of the subject of the painting, and, even beyond that, to its intrinsic sacredness.

I was not really surprised at Susan's words, for one of her own paintings hangs above our fireplace and serves as an icon as well. It depicts sand, sea, and sky, and, when we look at it, we look beyond it as well, towards the harmony and beauty of nature and nature's Creator.

When I returned home from Santa Fe, one of my first tasks was to check on the houseplants. A white amaryllis was in bloom and I drew up a chair and leaned close into the blossom, entering its world, so to speak. Then I went to get my camera and leaned in close again, towards the pattern of light green stamens in the center of the lush, curving petals. I clicked the shutter. Georgia O'Keefe had worked her magic.

Visual art is not the only art form that can illuminate our relationship with nature. Literature, theater, dance, and music can also heighten our awareness. When I was a teenager, one of my favorite recordings was Respighi's "The Pines of Rome." Toward the end of one section, "The Pines of the Janiculum," Respighi included the recorded song of a real nightingale. Some years later, I traveled to Italy and stayed in a student hostel housed in an old and somewhat run-down villa outside Florence. One evening, I stepped outside onto the terrace with some Italian students, to enjoy the night air and look down on the gardens, now a shadow of their former selves. Then we heard it. A song rose from a tall pine a short distance away. "Usignuolo" (nightingale), said one of the students. But I knew already. I knew because of Respighi.

Now, however, it is the French composer, the late Olivier Messiaen, who is my Kokapelli, although, as a devout Roman Catholic, he would probably have been shocked at the comparison. Not with flute alone, but with pipe organ and orchestral instruments, he enriches my understanding of God and nature by drawing me towards holy mystery through both haunting harmony and melody that often echoes the music of the natural world.

I remember sitting in the choir stalls at the Cathedral of St. John the Divine in New York City in a concert attended by the composer, hearing his organ composition "Méditations sur La Trinité." It was the only time I came even close to understanding the doctrine of the Trinity, not with my intellect, but in the deep wells of my unconscious self.

Messiaen's love for birds had a profound effect upon his music. The composer once proclaimed, "It's probable that in the artistic hierarchy, birds are the greatest musicians on our planet."[82] His knowledge of their music was phenomenal: he regularly intertwined their song, transposed to lower pitches, into his compositions. A notable example is his "Quartet for the End of Time," composed during his incarceration in Stalag VIII A, a German camp for prisoners of war during World War II. During his imprisonment, Messiaen arranged to take his turn in the military watches required of the prisoners during the last hours of the night, so that he could listen to the birds' dawn chorus each day. In the preface to the quartet, he would write, "The abyss is Time, with its weariness and gloom. The birds are the opposite of Time: they represent our longing for light, for stars, for rainbows, and for jubilant song!"[83] It has been said that "where all around him men were making war, Messiaen, like a bird, was making music."[84] Birdsong, which sustained and strengthened his soul during that apocaplyptic period, continued to be integral to his musical vocabulary.

I always wanted to tell Olivier Messiaen what his music meant to me, and, more than once, began a letter beginning "Cher Maître," but never finished or sent it. At a concert in New York one evening, my husband and I sat two rows in front of the composer, and I had my chance then to thank him, but was embarrassed to approach him because of my rusty French.

But one always has opportunities to make amends, and this is finally the occasion.

"*Cher Maître,*
Merci.
Nancy

Ponder and Pray

How have the lively and visual arts–painting, photography, sculpture, music, theater, dance–illuminated the natural world for you? In what way did they convey a sense of the sacred? List those artists who most have influenced the way that you experience the natural world.

Have you ever deliberately used any of their works as a focus of meditation?

Try doing so. An example is the use of icons in Orthodox Christianity. The painting is understood to be a "window" into the divine. But other works of art can also provide that experience for you. Perhaps it is one of Turner's great seascapes, or the waterlilies of Monet, or the or the bold colors of Rothko. Perhaps it is a Bach cantata, or Mozart's *Magic Flute*. Whatever draws you beyond the world of words into the mystery of God, helps you understand nature–even the cosmos–in a new and richer way.

4. Nurturing Hope

O joy! That in our embers
Is something that doth live,
That nature yet remembers
What was so fugitive!
The thought of our past years in me doth breed
Perpetual benediction: not indeed
For that which is most worthy to be blest –
Delight and liberty, the simple creed
Of Childhood, whether busy or at rest,
With new-fledged hope still fluttering in his breast.

—*William Wordsworth*[85]

For me, hope is represented by the two children whom you have already met in the first chapter. It is they who will walk into the future we have prepared for them.

They give me hope for several reasons. One is that I know that there are other children equally loved by grandparents, parents, aunts, and uncles, and that these relatives will have the passion to speak out on their behalf and on behalf of the earth they will inherit.

They give me hope for another reason, as well. Children can be our teachers, for integral to childhood is an inclination toward bonding with nature.

They teach us wonder, for one thing. When I taught preschoolers, I would bring in a pussy willow each spring. I would have my charges sit in a circle and they would pass it around, from small hand to small hand. A deep silence would descend. For most, it was the first experience of a pussy willow. Was it animal, mineral, or vegetable? It had fur, but it did not move. But it did not look like a flower or a leaf. Their fascination had led to contemplation, a useful progression for us all to remember.

I remember the flurry caused by my little brother's playful discovery of a garter snake. My mother and aunts, who were wary of snakes of all kinds, found him one day sitting on the front steps of my grandmother's porch, letting the snake glide through his hands again and again. I hope that their reaction did not infect him with a lasting phobia, although he has usually lived in suburbia and probably has not had many opportunities to test it out.

The childhood experience of nature requires leisure: unprogrammed time that is becoming ever rarer in today's world. Children need such "musing" time within the structure of their lives. It can be provided both in the home and in the classroom. Musing time is one of the features of the popular "Godly Play" approach to early Christian formation, based the "Catechesis of the Good Shepherd" developed in Italy by Sofia Cavaletti. After the teacher has quietly told a Bible story, all the while moving three dimensional figures or paper cutouts to dramatize the action, he or she poses some "I wonder" questions. "I wonder how it felt to be the lost sheep....I wonder how it felt when the Good Shepherd found you...." No answers are expected. The wondering alone is enough, a kind of prayer.

Perhaps natural objects could also be brought to church school–and public school as well–and passed around, as I did with my pussy willow, leaving plenty of time for some "I wonder" questions.

Better still, the children can be taken outdoors. I have a friend who takes nature walks with her two children in a woods near their home. After a few moments, she stops and asks "What do you see?" The three of them pause and look around. They notice details they would have missed otherwise, from small insects scampering along a log to the first small buds of spring on a nearby maple tree. Then they set forth again for a while before there is another pause: "What do you hear?" They listen, and once again, the sounds that had been obscured by the shuffle of their feet become apparent: the wind in the trees, the warning call of a distant jay, or the percussive rat-a-tat-tat of a woodpecker high above them. At the next pause, she might ask: "What do you smell?"–and they will discover the distinct fragrance of each season, from the spicy odor of autumn leaves to the soft dampness of the first weeks of spring.

Children are never too young to be encouraged to "stop, look, and listen," for such time for pondering is a catalyst for a developing intelligence and imagination. And no one is too old, either, for aging brains and spirits need stimulation as well.

We can also be mindful not to neglect the planet's own story, our "common creation story." When I present children's movement workshops about the biblical creation stories, I talk about the different ways that people have told stories about how God created the world. I explain that, long ago, people told it in one way, a way that tells us important things about why the world is like it is, and that now scientists tell it another way–a way that tells us how it happened. We begin by becoming the fireball of the Big Bang. I give the children strips of red crepe paper and ask them to huddle in the middle of the floor. Then I cover them with a large piece of red fabric and turn on the music (usually Milhaud's "Création du Monde"). At a signal, they "explode," throwing off the red fabric and swirling through the room with the streamers. It is all very exciting.

After we settle down again, I tell the Hebrew creation story from the first chapter of Genesis, first inviting them to close their eyes and try to imagine "nothing." Then, as I tell about the six days of creation, we "become" everything, often with the help of streamers or fabric, but most of all through movement. The most fun, of course, is the sixth day of creation, when the children have their choice of animals to portray–after I have tried to inculcate in them the concept of the Peaceable Kingdom!

Religious educators are becoming more and more aware of the need for materials that include ecological concerns. My husband and I were once asked to contribute to a religious songbook for children that would include not only traditional biblical themes, but important current issues as well. There was a particular need for some new child-friendly hymn texts about the environment. Fresh from my discovery of ecological design in David Orr's environmental studies course, I wrote the following:

> The earthworm in the soil, the flower and the bee,
> are part of God's immense design if we have eyes to see.
>
> Help us to understand all creatures have a part.
> We're not the only ones to be close to God's loving heart.
>
> The giant humpback whale, the tiny baby dove,
> are part of God's immense design for us to tend and love.
>
> The yellow butterfly who flutters tiny wings
> may cause winds far away to blow. There are no separate
> things.
>
> May we not hurt God's earth through selfishness and greed,
> or use too much of what there is when others are in need.[86]

My musician husband set the text to music; and, because the composer of a hymn has the privilege of giving it a name, we decided to call it "Orr." In the back of the book, there is an index of first lines. I smile when I see "The earthworm" taking pride of place along with hymn titles beginning with "Christ," "God," and "Jesus." Seeing this juxtaposition, I can't help but hear Mary's *Magnificat* in my imagination: "Thou hast cast down the mighty from their seat, and hast exalted the humble and meek." The difference is that, in this case, I am quite sure the "mighty" would welcome the useful earthworm, right up there on the throne beside them!

The experience of nature is a source of spiritual and emotional sustenance for any age, as we have seen throughout this book. It also should be an integral part of our education. We have always admired the fact that our son Christopher, after thirteen years in a stellar school system followed by two years at a fine liberal arts college, informed us that he needed "a different kind of education." He enrolled in an innovative environmental education program for his final two undergraduate years. Christopher's travels with the Audubon Expedition Institute took him from Acadia Park in Maine to the Everglades in Florida, then across the country to the Pacific. The program drew on resources as diverse as oceanographers, Mennonite farmers, and Hopis. Christopher is the new breed of "Renaissance man" that we need so much today, because his view of the world was provided by the balanced education he sought.

David Orr writes, "The aim of education is often described as teaching people how to think. But think about what? How is this learning to occur? If we strive to educate intelligence alone, which aspects of intelligence do we select? What about other traits, such as character, intuition, feeling, practical abilities, and instincts, which affect what people think about and how well they think?"[87]

Hope lies in education, related to a Latin word meaning the "drawing out" or "bringing forth" of what is already within a person. This education begins with the awe I saw in my preschoolers wide-eyed at the pussywillow cradled in their hands. It is nourished by our natural curiosity about the natural world around us, and our pleasure in bonding with it. This education is made ever more urgent by our discovery that all is not well with our planet. No less a religious leader than the late Pope John Paul II reminds us that this kind of education is also an integral part of the Christian path.

"All the more should men and women who believe in God the Creator, and who are thus convinced that there are well-defined unity and order in the world, feel called to address this [ecological] problem. Christians, in particular, realize that their responsibility within creation and their duty towards nature and the Creator are an essential part of their faith."[88]

Ponder and Pray

Do you have a young child, grandchild, or neighbor? Invite them to go for a "nature walk," which could be as simple as an exploration of their back yard. If you can go to a nature center, woods, or beach, better still. Have them close their eyes and ask "what do you hear?" Have them use their senses, just as we did in the "ponder and pray" section of the chapter titled "R & R" earlier in this book. Suggest things that they might look for, as if they were on a treasure hunt. Listen to what they say.

In an earlier book, I wrote about taking my little friend Davidas to the Bronx Zoo when he was five years old. In the middle of our visit, he invented an impromptu poem, which I quickly jotted down on a notepad. It went like this: "I hear the hawks calling, the birds singing, the feet of the animals. Nature is eating." Hearing Davidas's words, I couldn't help but think of the words of Sofia Cavalletti, the great Italian pedagogue, disciple of Maria Montessori, and catechist: "Children will help the adult to recover certain aspects of the message [of God] and to keep awakened certain vital wellsprings within."[89]

5. Prayer

Prayer the Churches banquet, Angels age,
God's breath in man returning to his birth,
The soul in paraphrase, heart in pilgrimage,
The Christian plummet sounding heav'n and earth.

—*George Herbert*[90]

When I was growing up in an Episcopal church in the suburbs of New York City, one of my favorite celebrations was Rogation Sunday, an observance which takes its name from the Latin *rogare,* "to ask." Like our forebears who walked the boundaries of their fields asking for blessings on their newly planted crops, we too sang a litany in procession. Resplendent in our blue and white choir vestments, we would exit the building where our Sunday School classes were held and march around the historic churchyard, singing the refrain of the "Great Litany": "We beseech thee to hear us, Good Lord." We would come to a halt near a recently dug hole, ready to receive a tree chosen by the ladies of the church's Garden Club. With due ceremonial, it would be planted and watered, and then we would begin our procession back to our Sunday School rooms. To this day, I can identify certain of those Rogation Sunday trees planted with such solemnity by our Sunday School.

I am glad that the church of my youth claimed a whole Sunday in order to plant in our memories the fact that we cannot take earthly abundance for granted. Our procession and the litany we sang were shaped by the understanding that our well-being was dependent on nature. We prayed for favorable weather, temperate rain, and fruitful seasons, as well as for a blessing upon those who work upon land and sea, and for those who care for earth, water, and air.

Prayers like those we sang on Rogation Sunday are but one way of holding the environment before God. We can weave our gratitude for the natural world, as well as our concerns for it, into our personal prayers as well. And there are many styles of personal prayer–perhaps as many as there are human beings. "How do I express my love of you, O God? Let me count the ways...." Any attempt to categorize prayer is bound to oversimplify what is deeply complex: our ongoing journey with God, who is both deeply present with us and also so far beyond us that our minds cannot encompass the mystery. But perhaps it is helpful here to think about a few of the ways of prayer that enable us to integrate our path of faith with our environmental concerns.

Certainly the saying of words, or *verbal prayer,* is one way, whether we do it in common worship or in the privacy of our homes. There are prayers "for the natural order" in many denominational prayer books, as well as several fine collections that can help us articulate our prayers for the earth.[91] But we can also voice our own concerns, confessions, intercessions, thanksgivings, and hopes through our own words, opening our hearts in conversation with God.

Both in common worship and in private, we can also

pray through *reflective prayer,* meditating on the Book of Nature just as we might meditate on a Bible passage. I remember once spending an hour or so at Maroon Bells, high in the mountains above Aspen, Colorado. It was a beautiful place named for the dark red bell-shaped peaks that loomed above a clear lake. I decided that I would walk and stop, walk and stop, over and over again, the way people might walk the Stations of the Cross by pausing at a series of depictions of the events of Good Friday. I sat by the lake, still as a mirror, that reflected the glory of the mountain scenery: the First Station. The lake shimmered, its calm mirrored by my own increasing calm as I gazed upon it.

At one end of the lake was a brook–the Second Station–evoking thoughts of journey and the willingness to move forward, after the calm of the lake. The Third Station, in a meadow of wild flowers abuzz with bees, was a study of the complex interdependence of all life, including my own, which is rich with connections with people and places around the world. A large rock, the Fourth Station, brought me thoughts of the eternal God, our Rock and our Redeemer. Quivering aspen trees danced at the Fifth Station, teaching me the freedom of moving with the wind of the Spirit. And so it went.

We need not walk "Stations" like this to pray reflectively with nature, but can simply hold an object in our hand (such as a seashell, small stone, or leaf), listen to the sounds of birds, wind, and insects, or touch the velvet of moss or rough bark of a tree. St. Benedict, in his rule for his newly created monastic order, called this process of reflection "lectio divina," and such prayer is very much like pondering passages of Scripture.

Contemplative prayer is the prayer of simply being still and silent in God's presence. Most of us, whether we were aware of it or not, have probably experienced such prayer in the presence of dramatic scenery, such as the Grand Canyon, a stunning sunset, or the infinite spaces of the desert or the ocean. One writer has likened such revelations of God's presence as listening to a mighty organ: "God plays on every stop that nature has."[92] However, gentler scenes can quiet our hearts and spirits, as well. Several times, my husband and I have visited Sissinghurst, a noted garden in southern England, often staying for a night or two in the farmhouse on the property. I would take the opportunity to just sit quietly in its famous White Garden, doing "nothing" but simply being in the garden. While sometimes I have found it necessary to focus on my breathing or on a word or image in order to settle down in this kind of prayer, the garden was enough. (I am trying to learn to do the same in our own garden, despite the fact that I am inordinately distracted by noticing its need for weeding, pruning, or watering.)

On my visits to Iona, I had a similar experience of simply absorbing the scene, "recording it" in my memory so that, along with memories of the prayers, music, and people I encountered, I could "carry" Iona with me when I left the island.

My experiences in both Sissinghurst and Iona began with

what I would call "extroverted contemplation," since I was focusing on something outside myself instead of within myself; but it led me within, to the awareness of God. That awareness can transform us.

Such transformation, to me, is the whole point of all prayer, and it is why prayer is an essential part of this book. The raw material that God wants to use for the transformation of the world is ourselves. Through our prayer, whenever we pray and however we pray, we are readying ourselves to become vessels of God's healing.

Ponder and Pray

Find a natural object, such as a leaf, a blossom, an acorn or a pinecone, and set aside at least fifteen or twenty minutes for this prayer that moves from verbal prayer, to reflective prayer, to contemplative prayer. Begin by thanking God in your own words for this time that you will be spending with the object, asking God to be with you as you use it as a focus for prayer.

Now, observe the object in your hand. Close your eyes and notice its weight and feel its shape and texture. Does it make any sound when you move it or brush against it? Does it have a fragrance? Open your eyes and look at it closely. Notice its color and its pattern.

Is there anything that strikes you about this object? Does anything about it remind you of your life? Does it speak to you of the Creator? Use your imagination to reflect upon what it might be "saying" to you.

Next, quiet your mind, and simply gaze at it silently, focusing on breathing in God's gift of life and your awareness of God's love for you and for all Creation.

6. Simple Gifts

'Tis the gift to be simple, 'tis the gift to be free,
'Tis the gift to come down where we ought to be,
And when we find ourselves in the place that's right,
We'll be in the valley of love and delight.

When true simplicity is gained,
To bow and to bend we shan't be ashamed;
To turn, turn will be our delight,
Till by turning, turning, we come round right.[93]

—Shaker Song

How better to conclude this book than with a song and a dance? Not just any song and dance, of course, but one that will summarize the theme of being grounded in love, and living a life that expresses that love. Its tune inevitably sets our feet to tapping, and its text is more relevant today than ever.

So let us join in the dance, a reconstruction by dance historians that illuminates the words.

The Shakers believed that the physical motion of "scooping" up the air in front of you with palms upward was effective in gathering up the blessings showered upon us by God. Just as our book began with noting the wonderful beauty and complexity of the natural world, the dance begins with welcoming such blessings.

'Tis the gift to be simple, 'tis the gift to be free':

Take four steps forward, your hands held in front of you, hands cupped with palms upward, making two small scooping motions with each step.

In order for that beauty to remain, however, we must shake off old habits and ideas that lead to destruction of our planet's well-being.

'Tis the gift to come down where we ought to be':

Take four steps backward, with two vigorous shakes of the hands with each step, palms downward and wrists relaxed and loose.

These first motions can remind us to open our hands and hearts to the world around us–God's gifts of air, water, forest, meadow, other species, other human beings–rather than letting them trickle through our fingers unrecognized and unseen. Because of the inevitable flaws of human nature, however, there are some things we need to shake off in order to preserve these blessings in the health God intends for them.

'And when we find ourselves in the place that's right, We'll be in the valley of love and delight':

Repeat the pattern.

Shaker communities were dedicated to simple living, gratitude to God, and service to others; they produced beautiful crafts, architecture, and many practical inventions (such as the clothespin) along the way. Their communities were meant to be small "heavens on earth," valleys of love and delight.

'When true simplicity is gained':

Step sideways to the right on the right foot, opening the arms to the side with elbows bent and palms facing one another. Then bring the left foot beside the right, as you bring the hands together, with palms touching, and bow forward, in a posture reminiscent of the Asian greeting that conveys mutual respect between two people.

'To bow and to bend we shan't be ashamed':

Repeat the previous movement to the left side.

In our middle chapters, we discovered that, rather than clinging rigidly to out-of-date attitudes and knowledge, we need to discover a new flexibility. We need to welcome the new insights given us by scientists and theologians, and to respect the integrity and intrinsic worth of each part of creation.

The conclusion is an invitation to hope.

'To turn, turn, will be our delight, till by turning, turning we come round right':

Turn in a small circle clockwise to the right, with the arms lifted up to the sides, the elbows bent, and the hands about shoulder height with palms facing one another. Then repeat the movements in a similar circle counterclockwise.

When we are flexible enough to change our ways, we have a chance at halting the course toward environmental disaster. Can we change people's hearts and minds in time? Can we learn a new attitude toward the created universe? Can we ourselves change our wasteful and selfish ways? With God's grace, the answer is "Yes!"

This hope is a gift to us, if we cooperate with the power of our God who has a long history of bringing hope out of despair and life out of death. From the legend of new beginnings after the great flood in the tale of Noah and the ark, through the great Exodus of the Israelites from slavery in Egypt into the promised land, right up to the death and resurrection of Jesus, this is God's pattern.

Once again, I quote Thomas Merton:

> For the world and time are the dance of the Lord in emptiness. The silence of the spheres is the music of a wedding feast. The more we persist in misunderstanding the phenomena of life, the more we analyze them out into strange finalities and complex purposes of our own, the more we involve ourselves in sadness, absurdity and despair. But it does not matter much, because no despair of ours can alter the reality of things, or stain the joy of the cosmic dance which is always there.[94]

When we become discouraged because we hear yet another dismaying piece of news and the message of hope seems silent, we need to remember the cosmic dance that is always there. Rather than turn in upon ourselves in sadness, we need to step forward, with our hands cupped, ready to embrace all the blessings of life on earth. We need to reassure ourselves that even our smallest actions, done along with the actions of others–while they may seem a mere shake of the wrist–can produce change when we do them together.

We need to be reminded that this great work is not a somber one, but a sacrament of joy that grows out of our love both for the Ground of our Being and for the ground of our *oikos*, our earthly home.

We need to turn, turn, and turn again in this dance of love, knowing that our movement can expand into a great wave of compassion and action that encircles our planet Earth.

This is coming down "where we ought to be," so let us all join in the dance.

Ponder and Pray

Dance "Simple Gifts" and teach it to another person, or to a whole group of people.

Appendix

Psalm 104

Bless the Holy One, O my soul;
O God, how excellent is your greatness;
you are clothed with majesty and splendor.
You wrap yourself with light as with a cloak;
you spread out the heavens like a curtain.
You lay the beams of your chambers in the waters above;
you make the clouds your chariot;
you ride on the wings of the wind.
You make the winds your messengers
and flames of fire your servants.
You have set the earth upon its foundations,
so that it never shall move at any time.
You covered it with the Deep as with a mantle;
the waters stood higher than the mountains.
At your rebuke they fled;
at the voice of your thunder they hastened away.
They went up into the hills and down to the valleys beneath,
to the places you had appointed for them.
You set the limits that they should not pass;
they shall not again cover the earth.
You sent the springs into the valleys;
they flow between the mountains.
All the beasts of the field drink their fill from them,

and the wild asses quench their thirst.
Beside them the birds of the air make their nests

and sing among the branches.
You water the mountains from your dwelling on high;
the earth is fully satisfied by the fruit of your works.
You make the grass grow for flocks and herds
and plants to serve all people;
That they may bring forth food from the earth,
and wine to gladden our hearts.
Oil to make a cheerful countenance,
and bread to strengthen the heart.
The trees of the Holy One are full of sap,
the cedars of Lebanon which God planted,
In which the birds build their nests,
and in whose tops the storks make their dwellings.
The high hills are a refuge for the mountain goats,
and the stony cliffs for the rock badgers.
You appointed the moon to mark the seasons,
and the sun knows the time of its setting.
You make darkness that it may be night,
in which all the beasts of the forest prowl.
The lions roar after their prey
and seek their food from God.
The sun rises, and they slip away

and lay themselves down in their dens.
We go forth to our work
and to our labor until the evening.
O Holy One, how manifold are your works;
in wisdom you have made them all;
the earth is full of your creatures.
Yonder is the great and wide sea
with its living things too many to number,
creatures both small and great.
There move the ships,
and there is that Leviathan,
which you have made for the sport of it.
All of them look to you
to give them their food in due season.
You give it to them; they gather it;
you open your hand, and they are filled with good things.
You hide your face, and they are terrified;
you take away their breath,
and they die and return to their dust.
You send forth your Spirit, and they are created
and so you renew the face of the earth.
May the glory of God endure for ever;
may the Holy One rejoice in all creation.
God looks at the earth and it trembles;
God touches the mountains and they smoke.
I will sing to God as long as I live;
I will praise my God while I have my being.[95]

[1] Quoted in *The New Yorker Magazine*, February 25, 2008, 52.

[2] William Wordsworth, "Ode: Intimations of Immortality from Recollections of Early Childhood," *Poems of William Wordsworth* (London: Thomas Nelson and Sons Ltd.) [n.d.].

[3] *Ibid.*

[4] *The Saint Helena Psalter* (New York: Church Publishing Incorporated, 2004), 166-67.

[5] Bruce Wilshire, *Wild Hunger* (Oxford: Rowman & Littlefield Publishers, Inc.,1998); following quotations from pp. x, 258, xii.

[6] Michael Reagan, ed., *The Hand of God: Thoughts and Images Reflecting the Spirit of the Universe* (Philadelphia and London: Templeton Foundation Press, 1999), p.51.

[7] Thomas Merton, *Seeds of Contemplation* (Wheathampstead, Hertfordshire, England: Anthony Clarke Books,1961), p. 230

[8] Brian Swimme, *The Universe is a Green Dragon: A Cosmic Creation Story* (Santa Fe, NM: Bear & Company, 1985), pp. 27-29.

[9] Elizabeth Roberts and Alias Amidon, ed., *Earth Prayers From Around the World* (San Francisco, CA: HarperSanFrancisco, 1991), p. 49.

[10] Thomas Berry, *The Dream of the Earth* (San Francisco: Sierra Club Books,1988), p.1.

[11] *Ibid.*

[12] Edward O. Wilson, *In Search of Nature* (Washington, D.C.: Island Press: 1996).

[13] Lang Elliott and Wil Hershberger, *The Songs of Insects* (Boston, New York: Houghton Mifflin Company, 2007)

[14] Emily Dickinson, *Selected Poems and Letters* (Garden City, NY: Doubleday Anchor, 1959), p. 177.

[15] For further information, contact www.earthball.com, or Orbis LLC, PO Box 1148, Eastsound, WA 98235, USA. (Tel. 360-376-4320, Fax 360-376-6050).

[16] *The Films of Charles and Ray Eames*, Volume 1: "Powers of Ten" (Santa Monica, CA: Pyramid Media, 1989).

[17] Gerard Manley Hopkins, "God's Grandeur," in *Poems of Gerard Manley Hopkins* (New York and London: Oxford University Press, 1948), p. 70.

[18] Lester R. Brown *et al*, *State of the World, 1996* (New York: W. W. Norton & Company, 1996), back cover.

[19] Roberts and Amidon, *Earth Prayers*, p. 70.

[20] Starets Zosima's prayer in Fyodor Dostoyevsky's *The Brothers Karamazov*, quoted in Anne Rowthorn, ed., *Earth and All the Stars* (Novato, CA: New World Library, 2000), p. 126.

[21] Roberts and Amidon, *Earth Prayer*, p. 95.

[22] Walter Russell Bowie, "O holy city, seen of John," Hymn 583, *The Hymnal 1982*. (New York: The Church Hymnal Corporation, 1985).

[23] Elizabeth Kolbert, "The Climate of Man–III," *The New Yorker*, May 9, 2005.

[24] Frederick Beuchner, *Wishful Thinking: A Theological ABC* (New York: Harper & Row, 1973), p. 95.

[25] M. Scott Peck, *The Road Less Traveled* (New York: Simon and Schuster, 1978), p. 81.

[26] Remarks by Seyyed Hossein Nasr, Professor of Islamic Studies, George Washington University, at the International Interfaith Center, Oxford, England, October 27, 1994. In Libby Bassett, ed., *Earth and Faith: A Book of Reflection for Action* (New York: Interfaith Partnership for the Environment, United Nations Environment Programme, 2000), p. 56.

[27] Lost Valley Education Center in Dexter, Oregon. www.lostvalley.org.

[28] Brian Swimme, *The Universe is a Green Dragon: A Cosmic Creation Story* (Santa Fe, NM: Bear and Company, 1985), p. 43ff.

[29] *Greening Congregations Handbook: Stories, Ideas, and Resources for Cultivating Creation Awareness and Care in Your Congregation*, ed. Tanya Marcovna Barnett (Seattle, WA: Earth Ministry, 2002). The following statements from denominations are taken from this handbook; the Appendices cited are found there.

[30] *The Book of Common Prayer*, p. 868.

[31] Jorge Pixley, "Exodus 20:1-17–A Latin American Perspective," in *Return to Babel: Global Perspectives on the Bible*, ed. Priscilla Pope-Levison and John R. Levison (Louisville: Westminster John Knox Press, 1999), p. 39.

[32] *Gates of Prayer: The New Union Prayerbook* (New York: Central Conference of American Rabbis, 1975), p. 351.

[33] Aldo Leopold, "The Land Ethic," *A Sand County Almanac* (London: Oxford University Press, 1949); this and subsequent citations, pp. 201, 203, 223.

[34] Bill McKibben, *The Comforting Whirlwind: God, Job, and the Scale of Creation* (Cambridge, MA: Cowley Publications, 2005), p. 1.

[35] *The Torah, A Modern Commentary* (New York: Union of American Hebrew Congregations, 1981), p. 543.

[36] William Blake, "The Everlasting Gospel," *The Complete Poetry and Selected Prose of John Donne & The Complete Poetry of William Blake* (New York: The Modern Library, 1941), p. 614.

[37] *Gates of Prayer*, pp. 154, 161.

[38] Abraham Joshua Heschel, *The Sabbath* (New York: Farrar, Straus, and Girous, 1951), pp. 29, 32.

[39] Frank T. Griswold, *Going Home* (Cambridge, MA: Cowley Publications, 2000), p. 3.

[40] James B. Martin-Schramm and Robert L. Stivers, *Christian Environmental Ethics: A Case Method Approach* (Maryknoll, NY: Orbis Books, 2003), p. 39.

[41] Anne H. Ehrlich and Paul R. Ehrlich, "Extinction: Life in Peril," *Reflecting on Nature: Readings in Environmental Philosophy*, ed. Lori Gruen and Dale Jamieson (New York: Oxford University Press, 1994), p. 342.

[42] Holmes Rolston, III, *Environmental Ethics: Duties to and Values in the Natural World* (Philadelphia: Temple University Press, 1988), p. 144.

[43] *Ibid.*, p. 158.

[44] Thomas Berry, *The Dream of the Earth* (San Francisco: Sierra Club Books, 1988), p. 11

[45] *The Torah: A Modern Commentary* (New York: Union of American Hebrew Congregations, 1981), pp. 557-58.

[46] Rolston, *Environmental Ethics*, p. 37.

[47] George A. Maloney, S. J., *The Breath of the Mystic* (Denville, NJ: Dimension Books, 1974.

[48] Mathis Wackernagel and William Rees, *Our Ecological Footprint: Reducing Human Impact on the Earth* (Gabriola Island, B.C., Canada: New Society Publishers, 1996), p. 9.

[49] Based on the story in Hans Christian Anderson, *Anderson's Fairy Tales*, translated from the Danish by Jean Hersholt (New York: The Heritage Press, 1942), pp. 79-83.

[50] Dante Alighieri, *The Commedia: Purgatory*, Canto XIX, translated by Dorothy Sayers (London: Penguin Books, 1955), pp. 218, 221.

[51] Alan Durning, *How Much is Enough?: The Consumer Society and the Future of the Earth* (New York: W.W. Norton & Co., Inc., 1992), p. 23.

[52] David Brower, *Let The Mountains Talk, Let The Rivers Run* (Gabriola Island BC, Canada: New Society Publishers, 2000), 155-56, 159.

[53] David Orr, "Liberalizing the Liberal Arts: From Domination to Design," *Oberlin Alumni Magazine*, Summer 1992, Vol. 88, No. 3, p. 17.

[54] William McDonough, "The Next Industrial Revolution", in "Weaving the World: Voices of the Bioneers," *Collective Heritage Letter* (Santa Fe, NM: Collective Heritage Institute, Fall, 1998), p. 1.

[55] Orr, "Liberalizing the Liberal Arts," pp. 16,17.

[56] McDonough, "The Next Industrial Revolution" 1-2.

[57] *Ibid.*, p. 2.

⁵⁸ Anne Rowthorn, *Earth and All The Stars* (Novato, CA: New World Library, 2000),p. 139.

⁵⁹ *Ibid.*, p. 40.

⁶⁰ David Kupfer interview with Van Jones, "Bridging the Green Divide: Van Jones on Jobs, Jails, and Environmental Justice," in *The Sun*, March, 2008, p. 8.

⁶¹ Celtic oral tradition, quoted in Rowthorn, *Earth and All the Stars*, p. 311.

⁶² Bill McKibben, "Measuring up." *Earth Letter*, November, 2003 (Seattle, WA: Earth Ministry) p.1.

⁶³ The *Didache*, or "Teaching," is an early Christian text. This adaptation appears in Janet Schaffran and Pat Kozak, *More Than Words: Prayer and Ritual for Inclusive Communities.* (New York: Crossroad, 1991), p. 51.

⁶⁴ Earth Ministry has been exploring the interface between environment and faith ever since 1992, when it was founded. See its website at www.earthministry.org.

⁶⁵ Michael Schut, "Why Food? Spirituality, Celebration & Justice," in *Food, Faith and Sustainability* (Seattle, WA: Earth Ministry, 1997), p. 9. This is a wonderful resource for those who would like to explore this subject further.

⁶⁶ Frances Moore Lappé, *Diet for a Small Planet* (New York: Ballantine Books, 1971).

⁶⁷ Michael Specter, "Big Foot," *The New Yorker*, Feb. 25, 2008, p. 47.

⁶⁸ Nancy Roth, *Organic Prayer* (New York: Seabury Books/Church Publishing, Inc., 2007), pp. 87-88.

⁶⁹ Willard Gaylin, "Sunbeams," *The Sun*, December, 2005, P. 48.

⁷⁰ Christopher Roth, *The Beetless' Gardening Book* (Cottage Grove, OR: Carrotseed Press, 1997): available from chris@talkingleaves.org or RevNancyroth@aol.com.

⁷¹ Psalm 19:1, *St. Helena's Psalter* (New York: Church Publishing Inc., 2004), p. 24.

⁷² Psalm 148: 3, 7-10, 13, *St. Helena's Psalter*, pp. 240-41.

⁷³ David Keller, *Oasis of Wisdom* (Collegeville, Minnesota: Liturgical Press, 2005), p.114.

⁷⁴ Hildegard of Bingen, *Book of Divine Words, with Letters and Songs*, ed. Matthew Fox (Santa Fe, NM: Bear and Company, 1987), p. 379.

⁷⁵ Meister Eckart, quoted in "A Sample of Historical Voices on Creation," *Greening Congregations Handbook* (Seattle, WA: Earth Ministry, 2002), Appendix A. This handbook, which includes several appendices, is an invaluable resource.

⁷⁶ Sally McFague, *The Body of God, An Ecological Theology* (Minneapolis: Fortress Press, 1993), pp. vii-viii.

[77] *Greening Congregations Handbook*, p. 26.

[78] Esther de Waal, *Every Earthly Blessing: Rediscovering the Celtic Tradition* (Harrisburg, PA: Morehouse Publishing, 1991),132.

[79] Alexander Carmichael, *Carmina Gadelica, Hymns and Incantations* (Trowbridge: Redwood Books, 1992), 105, 244, 337, 98, 120.

[80] De Waal, *Every Earthly Blessing*, pp. xiv-xv.

[81] *Book of Common Prayer*, 819.

[82] Olivier Messiaen, quoted in Claude Samuel, *Olivier Messiaen: Music and Color: Conversations with Claude Samuel*. Trans. E. Thomas Glasow. (Portland, OR: Amadeus Press, 1986), p. 85.

[83] Olivier Messiaen, "Quatuor pour la fin du Temps." Score. (Paris: Editeurs Durand, 1941).

[84] Rebecca Rischin, *For the End of Time: The Story of the Messiaen Quartet* (Ithaca, NY: Cornell University Press, 2003), 60.

[85] William Wordsworth, *Poems* (London: Thomas Nelson and Sons Ltd.), p. 340.

[86] Nancy Roth, "The Earthworm in the Soil," *Chatter with the Angels: An Illustrated Songbook for Children*, compiled and edited by Linda S. Richer and Anita Stoltzfus Breckbill (Chicago: GIA Publications, Inc., 2000), p. 6.

[87] David Orr, *Ecological Literacy: Education and the Transition to a Postmodern World* (Albany, NY: State University of New York Press, 1992), p. 142.

[88] Pope John Paul II, "The Ecological Crisis: A Common Responsibility," quoted in Appendix A, *Greening Congregations Handbook* (Seattle, WA: Earth Ministry, 2002).

[89] Sofia Cavalletti, *The Religious Potential of the Child* (Ramsey, NJ: Paulist Press, 1983), p. 49.

[90] "Prayer," from George Herbert, *The Poems of George Herbert*, (London: Oxford University Press, 1961), p.44

[91] An especially rich collection is that edited by Elizabeth Roberts and Elias Amidon: *Earth Prayers from around the World: 365 Prayers, Poems, and Invocations for Honoring the Earth* (San Francisco: HarperCollins, 1991).

[92] A quotation from William Stidger's essay "God is at the Organ," quoted in Robert N. Roth, *Wond'rous Machine: A Literary Anthology Celebrating the Organ* (Lanham, Maryland, and London: The Scarecrow Press, Inc., 2000), p. 182.

[93] *The Hymnal 1982*, Hymn 554.

[94] Thomas Merton, *Seeds of Contemplation* (Wheathampstead, Hertfordshire, England: Anthony Clarke Books, 1961), p. 230.

[95] *The Saint Helena Psalter*, pp.165-68.

About the Author

The Rev. Nancy Roth is an Episcopal priest, retreat leader, author, dancer, and musician. Her work as a resource person in the area of spirituality draws on her many interests: the integration of body and spirit, the contemplative tradition of prayer, the arts, and the relationship of Christian faith and ethics to environmental issues.

Her training has included studying piano at the Juillliard School of Music Pre-College Division, receiving a B.A. with a major in music from Oberlin College and an M.Div., *cum laude* from the General Theological Seminary, and life-long training in ballet and other forms of dance and exercise.
She was ordained to the Episcopal priesthood in 1981.

While living in New York, she was Christian Education Consultant at Trinity Church, Wall Street; taught meditation classes for performing artists at Manhattan Plaza; and served as Program Coordinator and Elderhostel Director at Holy Cross Monastery, West Park, NY.

Now living in Oberlin, Ohio, she is an Affiliate Scholar at Oberlin College and Assisting Priest at Christ Episcopal Church, Oberlin. She travels widely as a retreat conductor and workshop leader. She is a faculty member of the CREDO project, a week-long wellness program for clergy, and an associate of the Contemplative Project, sponsored by the Foundation for the Meditative Process. She has served as Chaplain for the Spouses of the Bishops of the Episcopal Church.

She is the author of more than a dozen books, which can be seen on her website, http;//www.revnancyroth.org. Among them are *Organic Prayer: A Spiritual Gardening Companion*; *The Breath of God*; *An Invitation to Christian Yoga*; *Spiritual Exercises: Joining Body and Spirit in Prayer*; and a series of meditations on hymn texts. She and her husband Robert, a church musician, collaborated in editing *We Sing of God: A Hymnal for Children*.

The Roths have two grown children: Christopher, a writer, editor, and organic gardener; and Michael, a professional violinist, who, with his wife Sarah, a cellist, has provided the Roths with two grandchildren, Gabriel and Anna.

3857494

Made in the USA